T0192374

Dramatic Storytelling & Narrative Design

A Writer's Guide to Video Games and Transmedia

Dramatic Storytelling & Narrative Design

A Writer's Guide to Video Games and Transmedia

by
Ross Berger

CRC Press
Taylor & Francis Group
Boca Raton London New York

CRC Press is an imprint of the
Taylor & Francis Group, an **informa** business

CRC Press
Taylor & Francis Group
6000 Broken Sound Parkway NW, Suite 300
Boca Raton, FL 33487-2742

International Standard Book Number-13: 978-1-138-31979-0 (hardback)
International Standard Book Number-13: 978-1-138-31973-8 (paperback)

Visit the Taylor & Francis Web site at
http://www.taylorandfrancis.com

and the CRC Press Web site at
http://www.crcpress.com

To Liat

Contents

Acknowledgments

How far I've come from being a penniless playwright in New York. Never in my wildest dreams did I think I would leave that city to do anything else. But when you need to eat, you'll go just about anywhere to earn a living in your craft. That adventure took me to Hollywood in 2006. Under my belt, I had one co-writing television credit, another paid but unproduced (and therefore useless) TV writing credit, and a bunch of plays that no one wanted to read. Certainly not the recipe for success, but I thought with my "New York edge," I'd have the cachet to get in the door at a television production company somewhere. Alas, no one would even take a meeting with me. The best I could do were lunches with assistants to junior executives … where I'd pick up the tab, despite my dwindling funds. Prospects were grim. Not to mention there was an impending WGA writers' strike the following year, so no one was hiring anyone that wasn't already in the Hollywood system … or wasn't related to someone who was.

I had to wait till 2007 to find work as a writer. It wasn't for TV; it was for digital content for YouTube. The pay was dirt (when there was pay) and the prestige was nil. Yet, it was popular. And it was the future. So I hopped on board. The shows I worked won Webby awards and got airtime on cable news networks. Again, it was the future. Video games followed later that year. Luckily, they paid more. And they were fun. I pushed forward on all fronts, writing for whatever new, disruptive technology was changing the way stories were being told. I figured if I wasn't going to get staffed as a writer on a TV show, I wanted to be part of the emerging media technology revolution. I've been lucky to work all across the west coast, creating content for new platforms as soon as (or before) they hit the marketplace – YouTube, iPhone, Xbox One, Oculus Rift, Google Daydream, and others that I can't reveal due to NDA.

I'm therefore grateful to those who gave me a chance (and the chops) to be a part of the revolution: Richard, Michael, Eduardo, Keith, Kelly, Mesh,

Miles, Greg, Ben, Eric, Dana, Robert, Tony, Rich, Jeff, Tom, Geoffrey, Jenna, David, Sean, Bay, Josh, Katie, Brandon, Brian, Jonathan, Niels, Andy, Matthew, Brittany, Marshall, Perrin, TJ, Yuri, Daniel, Ryan, and Sterling.

A special shout-out to Maurice Suckling whose work I've admired for a long time. Without his encouragement, this book would never have become a reality. Rick Adams and Jessica Vega of Taylor & Francis – thank you for your patience and your belief in this book. You helped make a life-long dream come true.

To my family & friends – Avram, Allison, Joely, Peyton, Rhoda, Vivek, Adam, Jeff, Barry, Damon, Yitzi, Boris, Sandy, Rhoda, Eric, Jody, Lawrence, Mark, Laura, Zachary. Thank you for reminding me that the difficult path I've chosen is worth it. And to my LA family – Leora, Oded, Yfat, Nadine, Joey, Molly, Mari, and my beloved Juka and Lacey. You were in the trenches with me, and I couldn't have made it to the end without your love and support.

Most importantly, I send my love to Liat, my motek, to whom this book is dedicated.

Definition of Terms

DISCLAIMER (SORT OF)

Most, if not all, of the game titles I mention in this book are published by mainstream publishers who have high budgets for development. Due to their financial resources, longer development cycles, and expansive gaming experiences, their games are classified as AAA titles. I omit any discussion of indie games, not because the quality of their narrative isn't up to par; quite the contrary. Games like *Journey* and *Braid* have made considerable impacts on the video game art form and are among the best games in their respective genres. Nevertheless, the thrust of this book is to educate fledgling game writers and narrative designers on what it means to break into this field, apply their craft effectively, and assure themselves consistent employment as a result. Indie games do not have the budgets to support a dedicated writing staff. Many times, the creator of an indie game will write the game herself. Or, she will hire a writer to perform a series of writing deliverables that is short term. Yes, there is more freedom to create what you want for an indie title. And perhaps you will sharpen your writing skills along the way. While these creative environments are fun, they do not reflect the typical daily routine (or reality) of an AAA publisher or studio. Most of those companies have business interests that greatly influence the content of their portfolio of games. More microtransactions, more co-operative play, more DLC, more live events – all of these put tremendous pressure on a dev team. The goal is simply not just to sell enough copies to make a profit; rather, the goal is to sell as many copies to become a hit, not just once, but for cycle after cycle.

Indie games don't have this concern, as there is little to no expectation of turning a profit. An indie game's goal is to be an exemplar of the purity of the art form and to innovate without corporate pressure or influence. One can break the boundaries by offering bold storytelling and brilliantly designed features. An indie game does not have to cast a wide net of fans; they just need a loyal following, even if that following is small.

In many ways, an indie game is a stepping stone for a dev studio to have their next game picked up by an AAA publisher. Or, have their current game get repurposed for PlayStation Network or Xbox Marketplace. Or maybe have a console version of their game hit the market *ala Journey*, *Minecraft*, or *A Way Out*. But those are rare opportunities.

If a writer wants to earn a consistent living in games, he/she must understand how to tell stories for AAA games. Writing for this type of game is the focus of this book.

GLOSSARY

The following is a list of terms I will use liberally throughout this book. Please take a moment to absorb these terms and acronyms, as they will allow for an easy shorthand between author and reader. They are also industry jargon and will be useful outside of the discussion of narrative design.

TERMS

Alpha: the final stage of the development production cycle where content is being added into the game. It should be the time before content is locked and everyone is testing the game and making slight corrections. In reality, new content is being added and everyone's working around the clock to keep up with the new additions. This is the most grueling time for a game developer, as endless hours, painstaking testing, and heavy revisions are par for the course.[*] This is the last moment to get things right, so one slight change to make the game better could have a downstream effect on other parts of the game. Everyone is working in lockstep to field these curveballs and optimize. Alpha is a pure grind.

Anchor Property: the central medium from which all other connected media originate. The anchor property is where game studios (or movie studios) put the majority of their financial resources and labor into. It is the main attraction of a franchise for a specific time frame. The transmedia extensions of that property include

---

[*] Some studios call this "Crunch Mode." Typically, this will begin sometime during production, long before Alpha. Nevertheless, the high pressure and endless hours in a race toward content lock are generally called "Crunch."

the media that builds to its release and then follows it to renew interest during a high sales season (like Christmas). Not to be confused with a *"tent-pole" property*, which is one of the biggest and most expensive products of a single company's annual portfolio of games. This term was, at one time, exclusive to the film and television industry, but now applies to video games as well. A tent-pole doesn't have to be the first product of a franchise; it could be a sequel as well. Its substantial budget is what defines it as a tent-pole. As a matter of clarity, all tent-poles are anchor properties, but not all anchor properties are tent-poles. An anchor property does not need to be one of the biggest media products of a movie studio or game publisher. It just needs to be the focal point of the transmedia extensions.

Conflict: the main driver of a story. Without it, there is none. Conflict is, in essence, an over-arching challenge that requires the protagonist to solve it in a set amount of time, or else the repercussions will be devastating. An antagonist is usually at the helm of the conflict, either by causing it or perpetuating it. Upon the antagonist's defeat, the protagonist can resolve the conflict. Example: a chemistry teacher is indentured to make crystal meth for a drug lord, who keeps the teacher's life under constant threat (*Breaking Bad*, Season 4). A Pinkerton detective must tear down a utopian society hellbent on purging the world of people who are neither white nor Christian (*BioShock Infinite*). An advertising executive must take care of his young son after his wife suddenly abandons the family (*Kramer vs. Kramer*).

The last example demonstrates that not all conflicts require physical danger. A conflict is about a massive dilemma that suddenly burdens the protagonist. The conflict might be small in the grand scheme of things, but to our hero, it is profound. If no action is taken, the conflict will be paralyzing and the consequences could change him/her detrimentally and irrevocably.

Cut Scene: an animated scene within the game that either instructs a player on gameplay mechanics or serves as a dramatic moment within the story of the game. Some will be interactive, as in, you can select responses to questions that characters ask you or you can move around within the environment. A cut scene is also known as a cinematic.

Dev: short for developer. This can refer to anyone on a product team who applies their craft in the creation of a video game, be they engineers, producers, project managers, writers, audio engineers, animators, level designers, visual artist, UI/UX designer, or another digital tradesperson. However, at some studios, a "dev" refers strictly to a software engineer. In the context of this book, I will use the former definition.

FPS: first-person shooter.

Game Mechanics: the building blocks of gameplay, such as how the game is played and what are its rule-sets.

Gameplay: a series of interactive experiences that ties a player to a game. What makes a game fun? What makes it addictive? These answers lie within the quality of the gameplay.

Golden Path: the central trajectory of the game's experience.

IP: intellectual property. This refers to any story, design, invention, and interactive experience that is owned by a company or individual. IP is used freely in the video game world as legalistic shorthand for the game itself. Oftentimes, it has broader implications and can refer to a franchise, that is, a game, movie, book, or TV show that lives beyond the medium itself and has an enduring shelf-life thanks to sequels, reboots, or other media incarnations (like comics, books, or animation).

Narrative Mechanism: one of many parts within the narrative arsenal used to reveal fragments of the story. These "parts" can take the form of a medium or device. Examples include: a cut scene or cinematic, a collectible item, in-game dialogue, user interface (UI) text on screen, a push notification through a companion app, voice-over during a loading screen, and interactive conversations with NPCs.

NPC: non-playable character.

Production: the stage of game development where everything is being built. Pre-production and the sprints beforehand are the blueprint phase with some foundational elements being built (like the vertical slice). Production is when the vast majority of the house is being constructed, fastened, painted, polished, inspected, stress-tested, repaired, inspected again, and varnished.

Replayability: when a completed gaming experience is played more than once. More specifically, you've played the game once through; now you're going to play it again, either to experience the same fun or to explore different paths that were not explored during your first go-around. (Games do not have to be completed to encourage replayability. A completed objective that encourages a player to re-experience it also qualifies.) Replayability is the goal of every game designer. From an artistic standpoint, it allows the player to experience additional gameplay opportunities. From a business standpoint, replayability increases the opportunities for microtransactions or in-game purchases to enhance a player's experience.

Story Beat: an event or action that either escalates or illuminates the protagonist's journey.

Story Milestone: a type of story beat that is grand in scale. It assumes that the hero has accomplished something significant or has experienced a major setback. Milestones include: Inciting Incident; Point of No Return; Low Point; Climax; Obligatory Scene; and more.

Vertical Slice: a playable level that is built during the last phase of pre-production. The vertical slice should include one of the biggest gameplay moments in the game and should have the best representative contributions from all disciplines – art, audio, level design, narrative design, programming, etc. If the vertical slice is approved by high-level executives at a publisher or studio, the game is then ready for production. If it isn't, the dev team will work to improve it for another executive review. If it fails once again, the game is at risk for being cut.

DISTINCTIONS

Context vs. Story: one of the biggest challenges for a narrative designer is distinguishing context from story for non-writers. First and foremost, context is not story. It is, instead, basic descriptions about a level, a new environment, an objective, or an accomplishment of an objective that informs the player of their progress toward a "leveling up" milestone or a specific goal. Context is crucial information that provides clarity and purpose for the player. Context, however, is not a driver of a story. How one conveys this information is often through on-screen text or even short cut scenes or videos.

It is therefore easy to confuse words on the screen or information performed by an actor as narrative. But context isn't narrative. It's news. More specifically, it's news about you, the player.

Story, on the other hand, is the overriding journey upon which the player embarks. Along the way, the hero learns more about him/herself, those around them, and the responsibility of the role they've just assumed. Context often has no bearing on the story; it can be easily removed. A player can figure things out themselves by moving forward and piecing clues together in their new environment. Story, however, cannot be omitted. Without the character's journey, there will be nothing at stake for a player to play for.

Nonetheless, writing these context moments falls squarely on the shoulders of narrative designers and game writers, mainly because our experience with words qualifies us to do so. Make no mistake about it: people will continuously confuse context with story. Therefore, always make sure to draw the distinction clearly and quickly before the rest of the development team sets expectations and detrimentally re-defines storytelling for their game.[*]

Plot vs. Structure: plot is the series of events that moves the story forward. "What happens next" is the appropriate way to understand it. Consider plot (or plot points) as the street-level view of a story; in other words, the micro details of how one event leads to another. Structure, on the other hand, is the 30,000-foot view of the story. Structure includes the major events of the story (aka story milestones) in which the plot is interspersed. Structure is the organization of events designed to strategically escalate the story. Plot is the logistics.

Publisher vs. Studio: a game publisher is the entity in the gaming industry that subsidizes the development of the game, provides development support in its production, and cultivates the relationships with the consoles makers (e.g., Sony or Microsoft) or platform distributors (e.g., Steam, Android). The publisher will provide safe passage of the game from its completion to its distribution. The studio actually makes the game; they own the creative experience. They will work with publishers to assure that the development is running smoothly and on time. Publishers will jump in and help if there's any glitch or potential slowdown of production. Studios though are the rock stars of the dev experience. The creative

---

[*] For a deeper analysis, please review my article, "Game Writer's Dilemma: Context vs. Story" (2018) from the *Encyclopedia of Computer Graphics and Games* (Springer).

vision and its implementation begin and end with them. Many publishers have their own studios, for example, Microsoft and 343 Studios (makers of *Halo*) or Sony and Naughty Dog (makers of the *Uncharted* franchise).

Story vs. Narrative: story is the protagonist's journey, inspired by a central conflict, where a series of escalating events forces him/her to achieve self-discovery. That awareness of self and purpose culminates once they accomplish an overarching goal or prevail in a final confrontation. Narrative, on the other hand, is the fictional universe that consists of a multitude of stories featuring related worlds and characters. For the sake of a single game, the narrative often refers to a single story but leaves room for more stories to be told with different characters if: (a) the game expands beyond its medium; (b) it offers sequels or prequels; or (c) it is vast enough on its own merits.

Theme vs. Premise: please check out *Chapter #3: Roles and Responsibilities* under "Reinforce the Theme."

CHAPTER 1

Introduction

COMING OUT OF OBSCURITY

Narrative design has been living in the shadows of game development for over a decade now. In fact, the profession was defined only in 2007 at a game publisher that no longer exists, that being THQ.* Beforehand, there was always narrative, but it was under the category of "Game Writing," which still exists today. (This book will later differentiate between the two.)

Even then, the writing responsibilities were seldom assigned to professional writers. Game designers took on this role with varying degrees of success. And the results didn't improve much when outsiders – namely screenwriters with zero game development experience or interest in the medium – were engaged by publishers and studios to write the narrative. In the case of the former example, the designer failed to understand the basics of storytelling and character development. In the latter, a screenwriter's ignorance of interactivity would make their work impossible to design around and would therefore be unusable.

The concept of narrative design is still being debated among developers today. *Why are they not just game writers*, as some might argue? *And why employ their services if story is often a disruption to the gaming experience?* Again, these are two significant topics I will address later on. But for the sake of this section, the dismissiveness by the majority of game developers is a primary reason why narrative design struggles for visibility.

Its adoption by game studios – and granted, adoption at a modest scale – is promising, albeit delayed. Big publishers like Microsoft, Electronic Arts,

---

* (Despain 2007)

1

and Activision (mainly at Blizzard) have been known to have their own narrative design departments or embed at least one role within a development team.

But story, as with any non-core game feature, is vulnerable to the appetite of the consumer. There are windfalls and there are droughts. But mostly, there are droughts. While no one can predict what a consumer will want, defining a unique, compelling intellectual property (IP) remains crucial. And cool gameplay moments are not enough. The competition will have cool gameplay moments as well. But story – that is, on a basic level: the world, the premise, the origin of the conflict, and multi-dimensional characters – is a massive differentiator for a product. So, it can be upsetting when story can define an IP, but those who create it are often not prioritized (or even included) in its development. Why narrative is not considered a critical role in a studio is, I hope, a momentary lapse of judgment. It will take writers and narrative designers to graduate to creative directors and executive producers to reverse it. In the meantime, the narrative designer continues to plow ahead with complex creative challenges that make the battle for visibility worth it.

Transmedia, which I will delve into in Chapter #13, has also struggled for acceptance or even basic understanding. The struggle is less of an issue of visibility – though that remains a serious issue – but more so one of legitimacy. Traditional Hollywood studios do not understand the importance of shared worlds and continued storylines outside of their anchor properties. Why spend financial resources to continue the storyline of, say, a supporting character? Any external media will be marketing and brand promotions.

Today, however, 30-second Pizza Hut commercials do not satisfy the appetite of consumers (no pun intended). For every *Star Wars* movie that's about to come out, you have millions of fans prepping for its release by watching *The Clone Wars*, playing *Battlefront*, and reading *The Screaming Citadel* comic series. The world of *Star Wars* continues to grow thanks to these other media.

To be clear: these other media extensions aren't intended to be marketing for big budget films. They are, in themselves, their own significant contributions to the lore of the *Star Wars* universe. They extend its mythology by adding deep, rich stories about characters we love. To deem them as marketing for the next big film is to insult the franchise. And it's this attitude that is pervasive in traditional Hollywood. Games, comics, books, animation, live experiences, amusement parks, and Virtual

Reality exhibitions – all of these are genuine, significant drivers of story. They expand parts of the world we already know or add new information that compels us to experience the other media in order to see how different parts of the mythology tie together. Why they don't get the respect of traditional Hollywood executives is because: (a) the big-ticket items are the films; and (b) executives don't experience these different media like the fans do, or even at all. Executives seldom play video games or read comics. Therefore, how would they ever know how compelling stories in these media can be?

Yes, it is Hollywood elitism that has prevented transmedia from hitting the bigger stage. But this is the old guard. And the old guard is dying. AT&T, the telecom giant, has acquired TimeWarner. Verizon, another telecom juggernaut, bought the digital assets from AOL and Yahoo. The beloved *Halo* franchise is about to become a television series on Showtime. *Halo* is owned by Microsoft.

These forays into the entertainment and media space by technology and telecom companies (and the list is rapidly growing!) represent a massive sea change. These companies see the significance of the changing media landscape and wish to harness it as a way to drive consumers to their most profitable platforms. There is no elitism here in terms of what the content is. Every medium, no matter the budget, is another prime opportunity to attract customers.

There is a glaring exception to the close-minded Hollywood studio. Disney's efforts behind *Star Wars* and the Marvel Cinematic Universe franchises are paving the way for a new appreciation of transmedia. The franchise planning behind *The Avengers* films is nothing short of amazing. Character cameos at the end of the credits foreshadow potential alliances in future movies; this shows Disney's commitment to creating holistic, enduring story experiences.

Disney has radically transformed the blockbuster film into a multiyear, multimedia experience. *The connective tissue that ties these parts together is at the heart of transmedia.* To dismiss its importance is to deny the massive cultural and financial impact it brings to the table.

In today's rapidly and radically changing media landscape, studios can no longer afford to keep the connective tissue in the shadows.

WHO THIS BOOK IS FOR

Over the past 7 years, I have been contacted by folks from various walks of life, who are seeking a way into the games industry as a storyteller.

Initially, those who sought me out were looking for a temporary refuge away from unemployment of traditional screenwriting. In the last year or so, however, the majority of the people I've spoken to are hardcore gamers who grew up playing games and still hit the sticks several hours a night. While they watch film and television religiously, their primary love is video games.

The disparity between the two is often generational. Gen X folks grew up with shorter games, both in the arcade and at home, but still considered movies as the central entertainment medium. Kids of the '80s grew up with 8-bit to 16-bit to the early days of 32-bit games. Those who stuck around for 64-bit games were fewer in numbers. But for kids who grew up on 64-bit games, also known as the fifth generation of video game consoles, the advancements of technology from that time (1993–2001) raised the bar extremely high. Graphics reached a new paradigm. But this was only a primer for the real gaming revolution: the 6th generation of consoles, which introduced to the world the PlayStation 2 and the Xbox. Such classics like *God of War, Grand Theft Auto II, Half-Life 2, Metroid Prime, Halo: Combat Evolved*, and *Forza* were not only blockbuster sellers, but were also highly rated games on Metacritic, the primary aggregator of all relevant game reviews in the marketplace.*

A new standard of gaming was introduced, and kids who grew up on these titles developed a kinship with gaming that had never been seen before. Those kids are now working professionals in their early 20s to mid-30s. Their appreciation for gaming does not come from a place of just wanting to earn money or to work temporarily in the field until a TV writing gig pops up. These people are passionate about games and want to make a meaningful, lasting, and profound impact on the industry. It's great talking with these folks. There's no hard sell nor is there a moment to justify why one prefers games over another medium. These individuals are sold even before the conversation begins.

I quickly discovered in my discussions with them that the most critical guidance I could provide centered on the realities of the job. Because, while games are fun to play, making them is a different story.

Generation X understands that challenge. Where they lack in passion, they make up for in sobering reality. They can easily detach themselves from the creative challenges ahead and deliver on corporate directives.

---

* ("Video Game Console" n.d.)

But they too need to understand what's involved in the everyday grind before taking the plunge.

This book isn't just for one generation. It's not about age. It's about devotion to storytelling in an unconventional medium for stories. And those devotees, whether they want to write games or just understand them as a way to fine-tune their own skill-set, fall under the following categories.

The Student

If you're in school studying video game development and want to pursue game narrative, then you will find that the basic requirements of storytelling delineated here are a good primer for your thesis project, internship, or first job. Or, if you're not interested in becoming a narrative designer, but are interested in all facets of game development, this book will give you a firsthand perspective of what writers need in order to succeed in the workplace. Perhaps you'll be well informed to empower your fellow scribes once you're in the trenches with them.

The Writer from Another Field

This professional writer is either looking to leave his/her current field of writing or trying to find a place in a related field that carries tremendous cultural impact. Many screenwriters of film and television have made successful inroads into game writing and narrative design. Some pursue it while simultaneously pursuing a lucrative television and film career. Others go into it temporarily to earn a living as they try to sell a screenplay or get staffed on a TV show. Some see games as an avenue to earn decent money while still actively keeping their options open. Typically, these kinds of writers are willing to write the content, but not willing to learn how to make that content interactive. For that writer, they will quickly discover that, in games, there is no quick payday. The work is too hard, as it's governed by strict boundaries in software development. They will also face the constant demand for making alternate content for the same story beats as a way to prevent staleness in replayability.

There is no phoning it in. And there is no working in isolation. A writer's work will have to go through a strict software pipeline – from writer to implementer to engineer, or from writer to actor to sound engineer to implementer – that will prove whether or not the writing works. If not, it has to be revised until it does. Constant iteration is the name of the game, and you cannot expect the work to improve through visual spectacle or an actor's performance.

Then there are screenwriters who are genuinely interested in the medium. They want to transition into games in order to pursue their craft and avoid the vicissitudes of Hollywood. If you love storytelling and don't care about the medium just as long as you can tell a great story, then this book will be immensely helpful.

The Entertainment Executive

For over a decade now, video game revenues have eclipsed those of film.*,† The monstrous demand is impossible to ignore. If you're a parent of a teenager, you can relate, thanks to *Fortnite*.‡

Blockbuster films often had video games released soon after its premiere. The games were either loose adaptations of the films or side stories of one of the characters. Seldom were these games ever any good, mainly because they were strict marketing ploys. As mentioned above regarding Disney, games are opportunities to continue the story of the world of the film (and *vice versa*).

A blockbuster IP can no longer afford to be expressed through one medium. Along with books, comics, board games, and amusement park attractions, games are the perfect next stop in the transmedia journey for a film or TV show. Games capture a consumer's attention for hours on end, many days a week, several weeks a month. Games are the perfect opportunity to expand the world of an anchor property and secure fan loyalty.

Executives are constantly on the hunt for the next movie blockbuster. If they wish to create a franchise – that is, a film that expands to sequels or has a life that extends to television – then they must learn to understand the impact of games and how a blockbuster film can expand the power of its franchise potential as an interactive medium.

Game Designer

For those who are already in the games industry, this book will dive into the elements of what makes a good story and an enduring IP. Game designers – those who design levels, systems, front end experiences, or gameplay – are often the closest collaborators with narrative designers. They must figure out how to balance the narrative within their features.

---

* (Chatfield 2009)
† (Shieber 2019)
‡ (Shanley 2019)

Game designers will often serve as points of contact for freelance writers who are working off-site. In this context, the game designer is intimately familiar with the details of their feature that, by the time they are collaborating with the writer, the task at hand is coverage. That is, game designers will know which moments in the game require dialogue, on-screen text, or environmental elements that communicate information.

Many times, they will write the narrative themselves and not engage the services of a professional writer. If that happens (and it is something I recommend against), then this book's sections on character, world building, and structure will be instructive.

Also critical: the sections devoted to what the role of a narrative designer and game writer is. This should set proper role expectations before collaboration begins.

Game Producer

Understanding the narrative designer's role as well as the scope of work will help game producers figure out how to budget for: (a) story development time; (b) freelance resources; and (c) narrative pipeline dependencies such as audio recording, motion capture, film production of live-action content, and others.

With this understanding, producers can map out the scope of work into deliverables that correspond to major development milestones. These deliverables should align with the duties of other devs to help determine when and how the narrative content can merge with other elements of the game.

Producers aren't always familiar with story development, so a deep dive into the elements of character, structure, and world building ought to provide strong baseline knowledge. Story development and resources are often on the chopping block when games get re-scoped. Gaining a full grasp of what story entails and how critical it is to the game's identity, as this book aims to do, will empower producers to make smart decisions on narrative deliverables.

Technologist in Media

Giants like Facebook, Google, Amazon, Apple, and Microsoft aren't only tech leaders; they're content leaders as well. Facebook and Google, while they have their own original content initiatives, are mostly avenues for a consumer's original creative output or for user-generated content. The individual can post a live stream on Facebook Live or write a post about the most random things and gain instant audiences through their friends. Google's YouTube is home to billions of videos filmed and/or edited by users looking to gain optimum views. Apple recently took the plunge into Hollywood and is now developing original screen content for its devices. Microsoft, on the other hand, has had a longer tenure than the other entities due to the Xbox and its proprietary content like *Halo* and *Minecraft.*

Technologists today are mindful of the need for content. In many ways, narrative can highlight features of the platforms they are building. Thus, understanding what makes a great story will arm them with the tools they need to optimize their platform.

Content Designer for Artificial Intelligence

If you design voice technologies like Siri or Alexa, consumer-facing software outside of games, or even chatbots, then you'll find lots of synergies with narrative design. Chapter #7 focuses on meaningful choice and branching narrative, which are also key pillars when designing experiences that help consumers find solutions to routine problems. Whether it's checking on the weather or seeking the status of a stock trade, automated services through artificial intelligence ("AI") are becoming a popular alternative to the human employee. Predicting what consumers will ask and then providing them with customized responses involve the same problem-solving skillset of a narrative designer. We are always deepening the layers of player interaction by writing, in advance, answers to the questions of the minutest detail. With every pivot of a conversation, we have already mapped out a series of responses.

Warning for Career Changers

Make sure your decision is well measured and reassessed continuously. Upon first blush, game development might seem like the perfect next step. Who can argue with growing sales, gainful employment, expanded annual reach, or increased cultural significance? Plus, it seems like fun!

Once again, playing games is vastly different from making them. The hours can be brutal and the demands can often seem ludicrous. Everything you've learned about good storytelling (or have been validated for, if you're a writer from another medium) can be greatly compromised during the development of the game.

Games are software. Software is dictated by software engineers. Creative is often held hostage to the demands of code. And story – being a subset of creative – is often held hostage to the whims of gameplay. In other words, if something is fun to play, the story can be butchered or stretched to impossible lengths to accommodate the fun.

But the fun is why people buy games. So, if you want to be a story expert in this medium, *learn to be adaptive*. The key to doing so isn't just about applying your craft; it's also about having the right attitude. Be nimble, be open minded, be respectfully forceful, and most importantly, be empathetic to your consumers. Adopting their mindset will dictate the majority of your team's creative decisions. If you're not on board, you might be working on the wrong game or in the wrong field.

Finally, my advice to anyone who wants to break into games is the following: *don't go into games unless you love games*. If that isn't possible, don't go into games unless you play games. If that still is not possible, then please – for the love of God – don't go into games unless you *respect* games. If you cannot satisfy this basic minimum requirement, there's no way you'll get hired. Devs can smell the holier-than-thou attitude a mile away. No one – *I mean no one* – wants to share the foxhole with either an arrogant tourist or an indifferent zombie.

But if you're the type of person that, at bare minimum, respects games, then pull up your sleeves and get ready to do some extremely hard work. Keep the consumer in your focus. And remember: if what you're doing does not enhance their enjoyment, then you're doing something wrong.

WHAT THIS BOOK IS NOT

This book is a practical guide to narrative design as a craft and as a profession. This is not a book that is heavy on theory. Nor is it a book that provides an academic perspective of this type of storytelling. Instead, I will provide key insight into professional expectations and basic how-to's to tackle challenges in the field. The goal is to properly equip storytelling professionals with the tools they need to succeed.

But, once again, this book isn't written just for gamers or professionals already in the field. It's for all storytellers. In the chapters ahead, readers will find a solid balance of references between games, movies, TV shows, books, digital series, and plays.

If you're someone who just got out of school or are transitioning from a related field to games, then I hope you will find that this book provides you with an honest depiction of a growing yet challenging field. Bear in mind: challenges ought not to dissuade you from pursuing it; they should, instead, galvanize you. In the midst of your narrative design journey, you will find that those challenges will make your job infinitely more gratifying.

Writing is an intensely challenging, often thankless endeavor. Getting paid for it, on the other hand, is a privilege. By the end of this book, I hope you'll have learned how to make the most out of that privilege once it arrives.

CHAPTER 2

Definitions and Distinctions

WHAT IS NARRATIVE DESIGN?

Based on the discipline's first word, you probably can gather that narrative design might have something to do with storytelling or, at the very least, writing content for a game. You're not wrong in that assumption. However, if it involved strictly writing content with no purpose other than to fill a screen, then the proper term would be "content writing." Narrative design is grander than that; it is also more strategic.

Based on the various games I've worked on with different studios for different genres, I have found that narrative design can be summed up accordingly:

> **It's creating a pathway for story, to be revealed one bit at a time, once conditions have been met, within or in between gameplay moments.**

Let's unpack this:

> **"It's creating a pathway for story ..."**

This is the "What" of the profession. Narrative designers must carve out a trajectory of the story. In doing so, a narrative designer must identify the moments where the narrative is intertwined with gameplay; what are the mechanisms that reveal the story (e.g., a cut scene, collectible, in-game dialogue, etc.); what are the rule-sets for those story mechanisms (i.e., how do these mechanisms work, what do they look like, what are the criteria by which they are unleashed, what part of the narrative will I be playing inside this mechanism at this given moment in the game?). It should be noted that all the basics implied within story, including character, world, and structure, are part of the aforementioned trajectory.

"... to be revealed one bit at a time ..."

This is the "When." Narrative designers must rely on proper story structure and dramatic escalation as a guide to parceling out narrative moments throughout the game experience. Then, the narrative designer will assign or implement those milestones to particular gameplay moments. Escalation of the story is dictated by the escalation of the gameplay moments on the golden path.

"... once conditions have been met ..."

"How." The narrative is not going to be unleashed willy-nilly. A player will have to: (a) reach checkpoints or objective completions; (b) achieve certain rewards over time; or (c) collect items that are natural to the environment. The result of these criteria is the unlocking of a fragment of story. What makes game narrative different from passive media like film or TV is that there is an *exchange between player and games creator*: a player must accomplish a task in order to receive the next part of their journey. Narrative is like a reward in the sense that a player must actively progress within game by using her/his skills on the controller in order to be rewarded with the next installation of media, be it new gameplay moments, narrative, or XP (aka experience points).

"...within or in between gameplay moments."

Obviously, this is the "Where." Narrative should never be a separate entity within the gaming experience. It needs to be embedded within those moments where players are hitting the sticks (i.e., buttoning on their controllers) and having fun. And players will do this for hours on end. So, the question is: how is the narrative properly distributed within those fun moments on the sticks in a way that doesn't take them away from the fun for too long? This is a never-ending challenge, and that's why narrative design is very much a strategic role in game development.

The "Why" is the story itself. I will dive into this in great lengths later on. Lastly, the "Who" are the characters of the narrative, mainly the protagonist and non-playable characters (NPCs) through which the player experiences the story.

WRITING FOR GAMES VS. TRADITIONAL MEDIA: WHAT'S THE DIFFERENCE?

One of the hardest lessons I learned during my first console game-writing experience was surrendering control to the player. Writers play God in traditional writing efforts such as books, film, or TV. They create the world and characters, and then they thrust those characters onto a journey filled with scenarios wrought from the writer's imagination.

Games can be the complete opposite. Players set the course for their own journey, that is, within the confines of game design. They turn left when they want to; they can enter different buildings upon their leisure; they can listen to another character or not. Games are all about player choice, which requires game makers to encourage player freedom while still offering those players a stunning spectacle, intense gameplay, and incentives (like rewards or bonus points).

Many games are "on rails," meaning they give little to no choice for the player and instead offer a proscribed, sequential experience with no variation. This is also known as a *linear storytelling experience.*

But other games relish player choice and provide alternative storylines and gameplay moments based on player decisions. In turn, these create alternative story paths and varied content. So, if a player walks into Door A, she will get a unique set of scenarios and gameplay moments. But if she chooses Door B, she will get a different set of scenarios and gameplay moments. Not surprisingly, this is known as *non-linear storytelling.*

Some games will "gate" or prevent a player from pursuing an alternative path in order to direct them back to the original path. For example, a player opens Door B. It leads them to a deep, dark chasm where the player immediately falls to her death. Yes, Door B was a different choice, but it was a false choice because it did not provide a tantamount alternative to Door A and instead provided a frustrating fail state for the player. Players crave variation and freedom of exploration. And both have to be meaningful. In other words, *not* a "Door B" approach.

If it is a sandbox experience (a game with a closed but explorable location for the entire experience), a writer's biggest challenge will be enticing a player to experience narrative when they are given absolute, boundless freedom to walk around however long they choose. Specific objectives are key to incentivizing the player to keep moving forward. Within the pursuit of these objectives, bits of narrative can be conveyed. But if the narrative is revealed through in-game dialogue from an NPC that does not force a cut scene, the player can easily evade the NPC and continue to meander. That NPC most likely had critical information that reveals more about the narrative. When a player ignores that opportunity, it is likely that the player was never a big fan of narrative to begin with. And if given the opportunity to sit back and watch a cut scene, the player would most likely skip it.

Writers and narrative designers cannot control which players will absorb the narrative. (Absorb as in "to accept or welcome," not "comprehend.") Games are about gameplay first. Narrative is often subservient to it.

That is the other fundamental difference between writing for games vs. other media: *players are not buying the product for your words*. Sure, the same thing could be said about a blockbuster movie with great special effects or a famous movie star. The difference there, however, is that the blockbuster film has a screenplay that dictates when the special effects go off and what the famous movie star says. In games, gameplay is the primary focus and everything else is built around those moments. Keeping the gamers' fingers moving is paramount. Games often survive without words to make that happen.

Prime Objective: Addiction

There's one thing you should know about this industry before you move forward: games are an addictive medium. Perhaps too addictive. But, in this day and age, they are not alone. Social media is also an addictive medium. "Likes," "retweets," and post replies from friends tap into our brain's reward center. Addiction to these media has spurred the establishment of Digital Detox rehabilitation centers, where people learn to manage their addiction through yoga, meditation, and mindfulness practices.

The science behind addiction centers on a chemical in the brain, known as dopamine, which is released when we react to reward-motivated stimuli such as gambling, eating, or thrill-seeking adventures. It's all about feeling pleasure, for which dopamine is responsible. And naturally, we want to feel as much pleasure in our life as possible. When we trigger dopamine's release at an excessive level, addiction sets in. It is hard to break the cycle because the desire for more dopamine increases steadily. When we eventually break it, withdrawal sets in. Negative behavior follows. We realize it is much more gratifying to pursue our addictive activities than not, so we continue where we left off with that behavior.

Games are addictive because they are designed to be addictive. Developers know what fun is and we create the mechanics to prolong that fun as much as possible. Slashing a series of beasts, punching a mixed martial arts fighter, or shooting an M50 submachine gun in 1940s Normandy gets the fingers in a near endless cycle of hitting buttons on the controller. There is tremendous validation when that enemy dies, as if to say your efforts led to something tangible. Moreover, you are a tough and worthy hero. The power of someone's life is in your hands. The more you destroy, the more rewarding it is (and the more rewarded you are). This reward-motivated behavior triggers more dopamine in your system. There is no stopping this behavior until the game ends. (And even then, one can look forward to downloadable content – aka "DLC" – and title updates.)

This is a lot to compete with for a writer or narrative designer. However, the mindset should not be how to craft narrative around addictive moments (aka gameplay), but rather *how to craft narrative that enhances these addictive moments*. As I will discuss later, the majority of consumers today want as frictionless a narrative as possible. If the story has no direct impact on the gameplay, it is often viewed as a waste of time. Therefore, the key is creating a reactive and proactive storyline that affects gameplay (proactive) and is affected by gameplay (reactive).

The term "addiction" is seldom mentioned in any meeting room at a publisher or studio. Not because we developers don't believe in it; rather, we just accept it for what it is: a byproduct of fun. And the more fun our games are, the more our players will play it.

In game development, it's all about enhancing the fun for as long as you can, for as many times as you can. Balancing the narrative within those parameters is not an easy task. Again, it's about minimizing the friction.

NARRATIVE DESIGNER VS. GAME WRITER: WHAT'S THE DIFFERENCE?

This is a controversial topic for us story people. The designer title holds a lot of weight in the industry, and many studios are loath to dispense it freely. Some feel that story people are just typing words and not crafting design documents that shape gameplay. That is a very naïve perspective of what we do.

In most cases, a narrative designer is the one who writes the fictional content that goes into the game, be they scripts for cut scenes, interactive dialogue trees, and/or environmental storytelling cues. Narrative designers often assist other creative artists in development to create specificity for a game's characters and worlds. Accordingly, narrative designers will work closely with artists and audio engineers by providing extensive character and world biographies that, to granular detail, give the other artists enough information to create 3-dimensional characters and vibrant worlds.

Game writers can take on these responsibilities as well, and, for some studios, these roles are interchangeable. But for most cases, the narrative designer has greater specialization. In addition to the aforementioned responsibilities, they create the story architecture, identify the vehicles that deliver story, design the rule-sets for when these vehicles are triggered in game, write and curate the story bible, plan and itemize the numerous story variations influenced by player choice, and lead localization efforts. (The following chapter will dive deep into what these responsibilities and others entail.)

The narrative designer's role is strategic, whereas the game writer's is tactical. Game writers are often hired after the architecture and the various categories of content have been cemented. They will work off a spreadsheet, designed by a narrative designer, and fill it in with the necessary content. These can be scripts for scenes, on-screen text, and in-game dialogue.

Barks

The latter is the most common task a game writer will undertake. It's a thankless, arduous effort if it requires redundant dialogue or chatter. This type of dialogue writing is known as "bark" writing. "Barks" give the game freshness to moments that seem repetitive when replayed or that take a long time to progress though. Consider, for example, the endless stream of dialogue when running through a battlefield and getting orders from a commanding officer to take cover. These dialogue variations don't move the story forward, but they add tonal authenticity to the moment.

This is often the lion's share of work for game writers and requires pure mental grinding. Typically, a game writer will be tasked to write 10 different ways of saying "Hello."

- "How are you?"

- "Welcome."

- "Good to see you."

- "Hey, there you are!"

- "Well, look who's here! When did you get in?"

- "I don't believe my eyes! Is that you?"

- "SO GOOD TO SEE YOU! How've you been?"

- "Well, I'll be a monkey's uncle. Get over here and shake my hand!"

- "Is that … no, it can't be … wow, it's been too long!"

- "Hi."

- "Hiya."

Mental fatigue sets in quite fast when writing barks. That's why the smartest strategy here is to break up the monotony by doing a set amount for one hour, then moving on to another category. Mixing it up, so to speak, definitely helps.

Narrative designers can write barks as well. But, it is often the case that they will be overseeing other parts of the story development process instead. While narrative designers will be responsible for identifying what types of barks need to be written and where in the game they will be triggered, game writers often own the process of writing them.

CHAPTER 3

Roles and Responsibilities

W HEN A TEAM HIRES a narrative designer, they are bringing on someone who fulfills the following roles: screenwriter, UI/UX writer, producer, director, content planner, game designer, implementer, localization expert, and editor (as in words, not film). They will help programmers, artists, level designers, creative directors, marketing specialists, actors, audio directors, producers, and project managers in their roles and responsibilities. When they are not wearing their creative hats, narrative designers will determine the scope of what needs to get written, acted, and filmed.

These skills are used primarily in the following categories.

ID THE IP

When creating a new video game property, the creative team (led by the creative director) should gather all the data from competitors, determine what's missing in the marketplace, and set a vision for the game on the basis of what kind of intellectual property the team should make. Is it ripe for sequels? What age group is it for? What demographic is it for? What's the genre? Who are the brandable characters? What are the brandable moments (that marketing can leverage to promote the game)?

Creative directors oftentimes go at this alone, but a narrative designer ideally should be there in the beginning, mainly because the questions a creative director is asking him/herself are questions that a storyteller has come across before. At this stage of development, a fully fleshed out story is not the end goal. Rather, one should strive to acquire the main ingredients to a successful franchise. These ingredients include: the world of the game; the tone of the experience; major characters; important weapons or vehicles of those characters; backstory of the characters and the world; and big-event moments.

The latter is key. These are selling points that a marketing department can leverage when promoting the game. Additionally, they are the north star for software engineers, artists, and designers. The larger the expanse of these moments, the more parts of these moments can be re-skinned or repurposed for other parts of the game or for future sequels. Big, dynamic gameplay moments are usually where you start because they are the most memorable and hardest to pull off.

Above all else, it is important to distill the IP into a single elevator pitch. What is a brief, but vivid description of the IP in one sentence, no more than 50 words? Consider these examples:

God of War (2018 reboot)

"His vengeance against the gods of Olympus far behind him, Kratos now lives as a man in the lands of Norse Gods and monsters. It is in this harsh, unforgiving world that he must fight to survive… and teach his son to do the same."[*]

The Last of Us (2013)

After a pandemic causes infected humans to destroy the rest of civilization, a survivor is hired to smuggle a young teenage girl out of an oppressive military quarantine. Their brutal journey across the country forces each of them to redefine their relationship to the world and to each other.[†]

Shadow of the Colossus (2018 remastered version)

A hero must walk among the Colossal beasts of a fantastical land in order to obtain their power. Only then will he be able to bring his loved one back to life.[‡]

---

[*] ("God of War" 2018)
[†] ("The Last of Us" 2013)
[‡] ("Shadow of the Colossus" 2018)

Succinct, accurate, vivid. The goal is to give just enough info to provide a hint of the tone, the world, and the subject matter while also providing differentiation from the competition.

It is imperative that the idea must be communicated in the simplest and briefest of terms; otherwise, the creative vision is susceptible to becoming obscured and convoluted. Game developers have a tendency to want to pack a lot into a game – not just features, but ideas as well. Successful games adopt the "less is more" dictum and let their succinct, but compelling creative pillars trickle down to every other part of the game. But if the creative cannot answer "What this game is about" in clear terms, the development will struggle.

Most importantly – and I cannot stress on this enough – the elevator pitch should not be a stale list of features. *You are creating a game, not a smartphone.* Think about character and world first before you think about modes. Allow the description to transport a potential consumer into the middle of your world. A list of features *will not* do the job.

HELP DESIGN THE GOLDEN PATH

Creative directors or lead designers often exclude a narrative designer in this process. But here's why that's a mistake: the golden path is based on a logical sequence of events that, by their very nature, are narrative in spirit. This isn't to say that a player should expect a cut scene to be triggered any time you visit a new locale.

Rather, a new locale will have an inherent logic attached to it. Why am I going to this locale right now and what am I to expect when I get there? Gameplay moments will be the main attraction to those locales, but the context to justify why they are where they are falls squarely on the shoulders of narrative designers.

Thus, the narrative designer's value in the co-design of the golden path is providing the logic, context, and escalating dramatic action that furthers a player's progress. The escalating dramatic action – e.g., the capture of a loved one, the decimation of a base, the death of a friend or partner, the seizure of a city, etc. – will intensify the journey on the golden path and should coincide with escalating gameplay moments. If not, the game will miss out on achieving optimum entertainment value.

ESTABLISH STRUCTURE

A narrative designer will have to figure out the end-to-end journey of the protagonist within the confines of the golden path. This entails infusing coherent and compelling story beats into the journey that will need to be closely hewn to certain moments on the golden path, including big events that highlight the gameplay. These are usually visually spectacular moments that are often part of the marketing of the game. They draw players in either through trailers, game review videos, or online screenshots shared on social media.

It is the narrative designer's role to make sense out of the big event moments, even if there doesn't seem to be any on face value. However, because these moments carry so much weight, they cannot be ignored in the narrative. They must be elegantly (or, at least, coherently) justified through previously seeded story beats.

Later on, I will delve into this subject more comprehensively, as structure is the most critical part of game narrative. Brandable characters and compelling worlds are perhaps the most memorable elements, but without a sturdy foundation upon which character, action, and stakes are built, there is nothing but un-sculpted noise.

ESTABLISH CHARACTERS AND WORLDS

This responsibility goes hand-in-hand with the aforementioned topic of "ID the IP." The identity of the IP can often be distilled into who are the heroes, the villains, the weapons they use, the vehicles they ride, and the environment in which they reside. I'll dive deeper into this in Chapter #5.

IDENTIFY STORY MECHANISMS AND DEVISE THEIR RULE-SETS

How the story is revealed is just as important as what that story is. But you will lose the attention of players with an egregious force-feeding of narrative through the traditional route (i.e., cut scenes). There are savvier ways to provide plot points and context without getting in the way of a player's "lean forward"* experience.

I've briefly mentioned dialogue trees and collectibles that happen inside the game and, later, I will discuss second screen experiences and independent media that are triggered outside of it. Whatever a narrative designer

---

* "Lean forward" entertainment requires the consumer to interact with the medium by actioning on the user interface ("UI") of the product. Video games, board games, software, interactive learning modules, interactive videos, and participatory live events qualify as active, lean forward experiences. "Lean back" or passive entertainment experiences, on the other hand, require nothing more of the viewer than to sit back and watch. Film, television, theater, and digital content are examples of these.

decides to employ to tell the story, they must establish the rule-set that triggers these mechanisms.

Take for example a hypothetical first-person shooter. It's a war game that takes place in the near future. You, the player, are armed with a series of futuristic assault rifles to mow down enemy combatants. You're wearing a smartwatch, which indicates how much progress you're making and how far away you are from reaching your next objective. The watch also provides you with directional information of the landscape as well as messages from fellow soldiers who are watching you through satellite.

In order to reach the next objective, you need to find an abductee and bring her to a safe haven – a newly claimed hospital by your military. If you kill an innocent bystander, it's a mulligan – you can continue on and maintain your rank. If you kill two innocent bystanders, you will lose your current rank, but still be able to advance in the mission. If you die along the way, you get resurrected and can continue where you left off. If the abductee dies along the way in either of the first two scenarios, you will not be able to advance. You must replay the mission.

Let's look at the two different results here, if you survive. If you provide safe passage for the abductee and have not killed any innocent civilians, you will embark upon a new mission with your current rank … or maybe higher depending on whether there's a level up at the end of the mission. This scenario would involve customized content. At minimum, it's a change of title in how you are addressed – e.g., "Thank you, Captain." vs. "Thanks, Sarge." At most, it could provide different, more exciting missions.

If you provide safe passage, but kill up to two or more innocent bystanders, you'll experience a suboptimal customized experience. At the very least, how you are addressed will change – e.g., "Thank you, Private." vs. "Thanks, Sarge." And it's likely you'll be set on a course to accomplish the same missions as the ones just mentioned, but the visuals might be different, less exciting. Or you have to engage in lower quality missions because your rank is lower.

The rule-set that allows the player to move forward is a system that requires different criteria to: (a) allow or deny the player to move forward; (b) recognize their achievements (or lack thereof); and (c) unlock awards (or penalties) and a customized path for that player.

How this narrative mechanism is triggered is part software engineering and part design. It also involves different voice-over, art, and sounds to provide the customized paths going forward. A pure designer will then coordinate how these different disciplines work together as well as integrate the non-narrative mission progression criteria within the narrative mechanism.

Now let's take a look at the smartwatch. The information that's provided to the player is made possible by a pure narrative design system. The communication stream – that is, the text that keeps filling the screen of the watch, including plot points and information that guide the player forward – is written and designed by the narrative designer. Design, in this sense, is establishing the criteria for triggering different information within that communication stream. A good way of thinking of it is given in the following graph.

Table 1 implies a certain order through which the player experiences the narrative content. Without a strong narrative design, the text will trigger randomly and haphazardly, mainly brought on by movement of the player character in the environment. That's why the triggers are so important to identify before the writing begins. A pure designer might just infuse the scene with narrative and ignore the importance of the order and frequency of the information. It's the identification of these triggers and their activation criteria that puts the "design" in "narrative design."

A narrative system, at its most basic form, is the underlying triggering criteria for a story mechanism. It requires the skills of: (1) a pure designer to establish the in-game, non-narrative criteria (e.g., achievements, unlocks, collections, progression in the environment) for the triggering; (2) a writer or narrative designer to segment which part of the story to reveal at a given time and to write the content per each segment; and (3) a software

TABLE 1   Narrative Mechanism Rule-set – Collectible

Text on a Watch	Is Triggered When
Watch out for the swamp. Serpents will come out of nowhere and bite you.	Player comes within 12 meters of the Gregarian Swamp.
You are running out of ammo! Find the nearest recon shelter to refill.	Ammunition is at or has dipped below 15% capacity.
This must be the abandoned warehouse where the Killian files are. Look inside and see what you can find.	Player has traversed past the swamp and has approached a dilapidated building.
The Killian Files will give us what we need to prepare ourselves for the impending war with the Etakians.	Player has entered the second floor of the dilapidated building.
Quick! Take out your syringe. The files have been laced with a bio-agent.	Player has opened the files. After reading the files for a beat, the player becomes exposed to a puff of dust.

engineer to create the programming logic to actualize the triggers and content in game. Art, animation, and audio are important contributions after the system is built and ready for implementation.

PLAN AND MANAGE THE CONTENT

Finding out what needs to get written is a crucial step before the writing begins. While this may seem like an easy task, it's not. There are so many dependencies that dictate what story mechanisms can be built. Budget and talent resources are the two most common ones.

The first step for a narrative designer is to draft a blueprint to explain what the story is. This could be in the form of a story bible (explained later on) or an addition to the Game Design Document (GDD). Second, you'll need to draft a visual representation of the overall narrative, potential variation moments, and the different vehicles (cut scenes, collectibles, in-game dialogue, etc.) that will deliver segments of the narrative. The final blueprint should explain how those vehicles will deliver specific segments of a story. This is crucial as it should dive into its mechanics and the rule-sets by which the story segments are triggered. This blueprint is not something you will need to do alone. There's a lot of software engineering that will take place. In fact, anything that is designed on your behalf will be scrutinized by a programmer for *technological viability*. Afterwards, narrative designers will create prototypes of story mechanisms to prove *creative viability*. Successful outcomes will impact the prioritization of writing deliverables. The narrative designer will then determine estimates of how much content needs to be written per each story mechanism, how many employees will be dedicated, and what kinds of external talent will be needed (for voice or film). This process will inform the development pipeline and expectations of delivery (i.e., by when, how many employees, technology costs, etc.). All of this will feed into the game's production schedule.

Additionally, there are many tech, art, and audio dependencies within a single piece of narrative. Figuring out the schedule, to which those other disciplines will need to contribute, will fall squarely on the shoulders of a writer or narrative designer. You will also need to "own" the narrative's full content delivery. This means you will manage and oversee: the various stages of the writing's creation; its enhancement by audio, art, and others; and its proper implementation and triggering in the game.

For example, imagine you are tasked to write a series of letters that gets peppered throughout the gaming experience and get collected by the player. (This assumes that the rule-set for the letter mechanic has already been designed and coded.)

A narrative designer will need to:

- Write the content of those letters

- Work with level designers to implement where in the game (as in environment and progression) the individual letters are disseminated and collected

- Work with user interface designers to figure out what is the best visual representation of the letter on screen

- Assure the letters' proper triggering for collection by collaborating with a pure designer and programmer

- Identify if there is music or voice-over (VO) associated with the letters, in which case a series of other requirements will follow, including casting the talent and directing said talent to voice the letter

- Assist with localization in the proper translation of the text of the letter (and/or VO, if necessary)

Again, not an easy task. Narrative designers don't just write the content and forget about it. There is a rigorous and collaborative process, where one must manage the content to assure its thorough creation and implementation. And if something isn't working after testing those letters in game with the help of quality assurance (QA), the narrative designer has to put on the hat of a supply chain manager, figure out where in the assembly line of content creation did that letter fail to trigger, and work with others to solve the issue.

REINFORCE THE THEME

So much of writing the story hinges upon the overall message you want to convey. It could be political or social. It could be about achieving goals that go beyond what we think we can do as players (and as characters in the fiction).

In games, the theme is a result of the creative vision. The story, therefore, must reinforce that theme through subtle means, such as: escalation in the story beats; visual reinforcement through environmental storytelling; context descriptions before missions.

A theme should speak to a higher ambition about the human condition. It's a driving moral statement or message. For instance:

- Honor, country, and self-sacrifice.

- Pushing yourself to the limits to surpass the expectations of those who don't believe in you.

- Becoming something greater than yourself by helping others.

- Learning to be a hero in a world where there are very few.

- The path to self-redemption for yourself and for your community.

- Family over everything else.

- Love conquers all.

Now, some of these might seem cliché. In fact, they are. Then again, there is little that is unique about theme. There are only a handful of general messages about the human condition as is. Theme is a guiding principle, not a series of plot points or character nuances.

One more thing …

Do not confuse theme with premise. As we'll tackle later on in the "Elevator Pitch" section, premise is a basic description of what the story is about. Theme, on the other hand, is the overall general moral message that guides your hero's journey. A breakdown is given in Table 2.

TABLE 2 Premise vs. Theme

Game	Premise	Theme
Call of Duty: World War II	It's the Battle of Normandy, and a squad from the 1st Division Infantry will do whatever it takes to thwart Nazi aggression in World War II's most decisive moment.	Honor and country above everything else.
God of War (reboot)	A warrior and his son set forth on a journey to honor the boy's dead mother only to incur the wrath of Norse Gods.	One can never escape their fate.
Shadow of the Colossus	A young hero enters a forbidden land of giants to rescue the love of his life.	Love conquers all.

WRITE, REVISE, AND POLISH THE CONTENT

The writing of the game's content is the primary reason why a narrative designer is hired. In many ways, this is the easiest part of the job. Once the story mechanisms are designed and the content plan is secured, it's time to write.

And you'll be writing different types of content based on the narrative mechanisms you designed. These could include mini-screenplays for cut scenes; prose writing in the voice of the game's characters for collectibles; mission descriptions presented on-screen; casual dialogue that is uttered randomly by minor characters as you travel through an environment; marketing copy to help explain or sell the game internally and externally; and instructional copy for manuals and/or on-screen tutorials.

The latter two won't be something the narrative designer is responsible for "designing." Nonetheless, team members might request help in these areas and you'll need to add them to an already-overloaded queue of work.

It's impossible to assess how much content needs to be written. This number is in constant flux, just like the game itself. Not surprisingly, it's also impossible to commit to a specific line count, due to numerous variations for a single sentiment (e.g., "Get down!" or "Hello"). For a typical console game, the amount of written content is often greater than a 120-page screenplay. That's not set in stone. But it is common. So, if you're a film or TV writer, be prepared to write a lot more than what you're used to.

As with all games, so much of the last part of the development (aka Alpha) is seeing how everything looks and feels in game and then making the necessary adjustments. Some of these adjustments could include wholesale changes on what is written inside an already-secured narrative mechanism. Take, for example, the aforementioned letter collectible. The individual letters and their placement in the game will be scrutinized *ad nauseum*. If the change recommendations are merely cosmetic, you're in luck. (Example: change the word "haunting" to "foreboding.") But, if the letters tested poorly with focus groups due to lack of coherence, then a narrative designer must provide deep writing revisions and (if need be) work with a pure designer to re-implement them in different points in the game. However, such changes are only permitted if the narrative mechanism that needs fixing is not already carved in stone or is too expensive to change at the last minute. Cut scenes, for instance, are too expensive and rigid. But collectibles or dialogue trees –

since they do not require heavy animations, VO, or motion capture (aka MOCAP) – are the most vulnerable and easiest to change.

As Ernest Hemingway once wrote, "The only kind of writing is rewriting." Yes, you will be busy revising. But so will everyone else. Polishing features, re-tuning the frequency of certain character appearances, fixing bugs in code – all of these and more are compounded during crunch mode. This is game development. Expect nothing less than an all-hands-on-deck approach to perfecting the product until content is locked.

ASSIST IN THE LOCALIZATION OF THE WRITTEN AND SPOKEN CONTENT

The video game industry is massive in part because it is a global industry. More and more people have access to technology than ever before and often have more than one device through which they play games. Phones, tablets, consoles, computers, virtual reality headsets – games are omnipresent. Game companies realize that, to spread consumer goodwill across the world, it is a *must* to translate VO subtitles and on-screen text into numerous languages.

There are whole departments in video game companies devoted to translation of this content. This process is known as localization and it requires not just the straight word-for-word translation from one language to the next, but an actual cultural translation as well. For instance, an off-handed insult in English about one's lack of Americanism ("You red-diaper, Commie bastard") will need to be translated into one of the many Chinese languages that does not offend the country's political or familial sensibilities. A more appropriate translation could be, for example, "You disrespectful, treasonous simpleton."

Narrative designers are key to the localization process. While they will not translate the materials, they will instead prepare all of the materials that need to get translated. Additionally, they will input the content into a translation tool, monitor the changes that affect the translations, and make the proper revisions and updates so that the localization team is aware of what new content they need to translate.

Localization is a very time-consuming process that occurs near the end of the development of a game. The work is often thankless, but it is critical. It is, really, the final step in making sure that a writer's words truly reach a large audience.

DIRECT VOICE-OVER SESSIONS AND FILMED CONTENT

Voice-Over

Voice-over is a common component to games. Even if there is no story, *per se*, actors are often used to provide ambient dialogue to a scene in order to add authenticity. In a sports game, for instance, broadcasters react to any and all moves that the player conducts on the court, field, or ring. That extra layer of authenticity gives players a deeper connection to the game.

Outside of the sports arena, ambient dialogue again provides that extra layer of believability. Even if the game is sci-fi, hearing a nearby soldier kill a Lekgolo will force you to follow him into the next spaceship, which enhances the intensity and suspense of the moment.

Voice-over without narrative can also provide essential context to features in the game. A voice from an off-screen character that guides you through tutorials and character customization or provides descriptions of modes or features before you play them gives the player the necessary information on how to proceed. Without that VO, the player would have to fend for himself/herself. And, if there's one thing game developers do not want to do it is to frustrate or slow down a player in experiencing fun.

But, most importantly, VO actors provide the performances that enhance and communicate the narrative. Their performances are often the voice of in-game characters that are either motion captured or just purely animated. Sometimes, there is no on-screen character that they are voicing. Instead, an off-screen Voice of God character is a common motif for games, especially for those with a limited character-animation budget. These characters will guide the player through the experience, not just as a provider of context, but as a person who watches over the player. These Voice of God characters typically serve as a parental figure, friend, or mentor.*

No matter the role, the narrative designer must have a strong command of the characters' intentions, roles, and other details that can be used to inform the actor's performance. When the actors are in the sound booth, you must be hyper-aware of their performance. Is it providing the right intention? Is it true to the character you created? You'll need to adopt basic directorial responsibilities to assure the high quality of the performance.

If there is already a director assigned to the VO sessions, then the narrative designer's role includes the following: (1) making sure the lines are

---

* GlaDOS in the first *Portal* (2007) game is a perfect example … although when her true intentions are revealed, she is neither a parental figure, friend, nor mentor. She's just a cold AI seeking to end your existence. Still, her presence is mostly off-screen as a Voice of God character.

properly performed and influenced by the sequence of events in the game; (2) maintaining the integrity of the script if there are ad-libs from the actor that could compromise the accuracy of the story; (3) rewriting lines if the actors are having a hard time with the direction or with what's written; (4) assuring everything is delivered within a certain time constraint per line, if such a constraint exists (which it can); and (5) consulting with the director to assure high-quality performances without being intrusive. The latter seems like common sense, but you'd be surprised at how many writers and narrative designers ignore that rule. It's often the case that many of these writers have never worked with actors before, so they have yet to learn the rules of etiquette that govern the relationship between actor, director, sound engineer, and writer.

Voice-over sessions do not happen regularly; therefore, the time in the sound booth is precious. If a writer doesn't have his/her ducks in a row – as in, they do not have all of the content written that needs to be recorded or they want to add too much unnecessary content just for extra coverage – the actor's performance will deteriorate quickly. Voice-over sessions, ideally, should be about getting the best performance possible out of an actor. It should not be about figuring out stuff on the fly or adding more to the plate than is needed. Content that is "nice to have" can often ruin a VO session. Solidify those nice-to-haves at least a week before the recording and prioritize accordingly.

Filmed Content

Cut scenes, as referenced earlier, are animated scenes within the game that move the story forward and provide greater context to the world and characters. Gamers can find these moments disruptive if the cut scenes are not interactive (and most of the time they aren't). Cut scenes are skippable, and many gamers take advantage of that function to get to gameplay as quickly as possible. But for those who want to experience everything a game has to offer, cut scenes are a game's version of cinema.

The animation process involves the capturing of an actor's facial gestures and body structure. This is done through a process known as motion capture or MOCAP. Actors will wear a suit and facial markers that serve as a scanner of an actor's unique subtle movements and skeletal structure. The suit and markers are basically data receptors that are activated by a series of cameras spread throughout a stage or studio.* A single camera's

---

* ("Motion Capture" n.d.)

positioning will differ from another, but its goal is to capture structural and skeletal pieces of data that a body and/or body part gives off. Since our bodies are so complex and filled with nuance thanks to our 650+ muscles and 200+ bones, more cameras will capture more data of an actor's body and movement. The more the data, the greater the authenticity of the actor's representation in an animated form.

Narrative designers and writers are not responsible for the process of MOCAP, but they will be responsible for writing the scenes that need to be performed and captured. Cut scenes are opportunities for actors to perform at their highest level. The subtleties of their facial expressions will need to be captured and done so thoroughly. Otherwise, an improper facial expression could undermine the tone and content of a sentence. Narrative designers and writers can direct or assist in the directing of these scenes. However, it is often the case – especially at big studios for big-budget games – that a director who specializes in MOCAP will take the reins. The writer will be a crucial contributor, not only to help communicate the intention of the scene, but to educate the actors on what the consequences of that scene will be in gameplay.

A false step from a performance will yield imperfect animation data. This will kill a cut scene. Scenes will have different takes that are recorded, so the creative team does have an opportunity to choose which data-driven shots work best for a scene. However, a writer cannot rely on too many takes. While MOCAP is expensive, it's even more so arduous and physically demanding. Actors are wearing suits that are not breathable. Facial markers are susceptible to falling off or breaking, thus preventing accurate data from being captured. Time is short, so make sure you know what to communicate to an actor before the MOCAP begins.

While animation is the predominant form of character representation, some games rely on traditional live-action film to fuel the narrative. These are known as FMVs, or full motion videos. FMVs' popularity peaked in the 1990s with game versions of such famous franchises as *The X-Files* and *Star Trek*. But they are used sparingly today and usually as a way to provide cameos of well-established personalities to add authenticity to the world of the game. Sports games are the perfect genre for this. Seeing a live-action version of a superstar, sportscaster, or coach that talks about the player (as if the content was customized to them) can be an effective addition to the experience.

If FMV is part of the game, a writer will need to think of it as traditional film production. The actors' performances cannot be fixed through animation. Therefore, expect a degree of finality when working on a film set. If you lack film production experience, rely on those who do have it and make sure to be a watchdog for the story. If an ad lib or improper interpretation of a line could undermine the narrative or subsequent gameplay moments, be ready to provide instant feedback by working through the director.

OTHER

When a game is in crunch, new roles and responsibilities will be thrown at everyone. It's an "all-hands-on-deck" situation; taking on more than what your job description entails is *de rigueur*. A narrative designer will be asked to help edit designer's tutorials or guidance content; they will work with the marketing department to write about certain features of the game for print and digital outlets; they will work with key stakeholders in drafting or updating game manuals (yes, they still exist, albeit digitally); they will work with a UI team to help reword on-screen content to fit the needs of an updated user interface; they will work with an art team to provide information on characters or locales to assist that team in getting a better visual picture of the task at hand; and they will work with engineers to write software notes for title updates.

For better or worse, a narrative designer is the editorial subject matter expert of a game development team, and will field requests that have nothing to do with story. Proper mastery of grammar, vocabulary, semantics, and sentence structure is constantly in need. If a writer is soft in these areas, he/she will need to fine-tune that skill-set *ex post haste*.

CHAPTER 4

Game Writing at the Ground Level

T HERE'S A LOT OF prep work during the early stages of the game. Character bios, world bios, sample dialogue, sample scenes, a vertical slice script, and more are written in a standard doc form *ala* Microsoft Word or Google Docs. They are great pre-production tools and allow the writer to write unencumbered. An empty canvas to be filled with your words is extremely empowering. However, once the game is in production, writers will have to make huge compromises on their process.

EXAMPLE SPREADSHEET FOR NARRATIVE CONTENT

The heavy demands of production require a game writer or narrative designer to work almost exclusively in a spreadsheet. The transference of data – and yes, at this stage, narrative content, like dialogue, is data – will go through several different hands from several different specialists including designers, audio engineers, localization specialists, and quality assurance analysts.

It's imperative that the information in these spreadsheets provides the most comprehensive, up-to-date data so that the above stakeholders won't miss anything once applying their trade. Missing data or mis-informed data can create bugs with serious downstream effects that can slowdown production.

Asset ID	Category	Character	Line	Character Count	Notes
Library_Hero_001a_Male	Murder Investigation in Library	Smith	Hello -- may I bend your ear for a sec?	39	Informal path. Not sure we can pay off. Check out latest update to character bible.
Library_Hero_001b_Male	Murder Investigation in Library	Smith	Hey, were you here during last night's murder?	46	
Library_Hero_001c_Male	Murder Investigation in Library	Smith	I need to ask you some questions.	33	
Library_Hero_001a_Female	Murder Investigation in Library	Smith	Hi there -- do you have a moment?	33	
Library_Hero_001b_Female	Murder Investigation in Library	Smith	Sorry to bother. Just need to ask you some questions about last night's murder.	79	
Library_Hero_001c_Female	Murder Investigation in Library	Smith	Excuse me. I need a moment of your time. Right now.	51	
Library_Librarian_001_Male	Murder Investigation in Library	Chen	Of course. How can I help you?	30	
Library_Librarian_001_Female	Murder Investigation in Library	Chen	Of course. How can I help you?	30	

FIGURE 1   Spreadsheet for Writing Game Content. (See full-scale version of this graph at www.crcpress.com/9781138319738.)

Figure 1 is a bare-bones example of a spreadsheet that a writer would typically contribute to. Let me describe in detail what each column means.

ASSET ID

Under Column A, the data refer to an asset identifier. If this line is either voiced or represented through in-game text, the narrative designer will affix this asset ID to the asset type (in this case, in-game text), so that a pure designer knows what asset they are implementing into the game. If it's an asset that is voice-over, audio engineers will use the asset ID as a way to track progress of their polishing and implementing of that voiced line.

Once it's out of the hands of a pure designer or audio team, the localization team can then translate that asset into various languages and provide the subsequent subtitles for it.

The quality assurance team can also refer to the asset ID in case the exact representation of the asset ID pops up as a string instead of the in-game text. In other words, what pops up on screen is "Library_Hero_001a_Male" instead of "Hello – may I bend your ear for a sec?" Then they can report a bug to the designer to see what went wrong in the implementation process.

Let's breakdown the data in the asset ID itself. Going back to the first line: "Library_Hero_001a_Male." There's a lot there in just a few characters. Ideal nomenclature for the identifier should provide: the location in the game environment that the line is stated in ("Library_"); the person who is uttering the line ("_Hero_"); which line in the series of lines in that scene that the same character is uttering ("_001"); the version of that line, in case variations are written ("a"); and the gender of the speaker of that line in case, once again, there are different versions of that same character ("_Male").

Each team has different rules under which the nomenclature of the asset ID is written, but the goal is to clarify who the line came from, where it took place, and what the numeric or alphabetic distinctions are if there are variations of that same line. And the last challenge: make the asset ID as economical as you can. The tools that allow for the implementation usually display an enormous list of IDs that need to get put in game. Oftentimes, reading a huge list of these can strain the eyes and increase the chance of human error. Longer nomenclature will compound that likelihood.

This can be hard to adjust to at first, but will make sense eventually once you're charged with adding several variations for a single line. The artificial intelligence (AI) of the game could trigger any one of these three lines (_001a, _001b, or _001c) if you are the Male Hero Smith as an introduction to the conversation, so make sure the appropriate variant corresponds with the appropriate asset ID.

If you are the Female Hero Smith, the AI will launch one of the three – Library_Hero_001a_Female, Library_Hero_001b_Female, or Library_Hero_001c_Female – for the same introduction that involved the Male Hero Smith.

Now these lines of dialogue could be the same – and that is likely the case when a writer or narrative designer writes this scene. Nonetheless, the lines will need to have separate asset IDs (mainly influenced by gender) so that they are properly translated once these IDs are in the hands of localization.

CATEGORY

Here, the type of scene needs to be communicated, so that the writer has an understanding of when, in the game, this part of the narrative is delivered. The near equivalent of this in a typical screenplay would be stage directions.

The Category column also refers to the type of moment that gets triggered that is independent of the story. Barks, as mentioned earlier, are the perfect candidates for this. Their criteria could be as simple as 27 different ways of saying "hello." But a different rule-set, event, or environment could dictate how, where, or when these barks are triggered and (sometimes) performed. For example, you collected an item. If the collection mechanic is common, but as common as a greeting like "Hello," you will need to account for *all the variations* of that type of line under the "Category" column.

CHARACTER

This is pretty straightforward and sometimes redundant if the name of the character is already embedded in the asset ID. However, it's most useful in the aggregation of the lines for a specific character. If a wholesale rewrite is needed (for instance, Chen is no longer a librarian, but a construction worker) or if the lines need to be grouped for a voice-over session, a simple function on the spreadsheet can easily organize the data in the "Character" field.

LINE

Another straightforward column. But it is here where writers and narrative designers will do their most work, either through the creation of the lines or the editing of them. Pure designers will import the spreadsheet into a database that will then be imported into the game's engine in order for the new dialogue to be present in the game. Again, designers might have a different setup of the spreadsheet to make the transference as seamless as possible.

The same method applies when importing this information into a database for localization.

CHARACTER COUNT

One of the biggest challenges for a writer in video games is writing under the constraints of a character count. Dialogue, at its best, is unfettered. But when writing for an audience, unfettered dialogue can go on for too long; that's why it's critical that the dialogue remains taut while still revealing character psychology and crucial information.

But games can get fascist when it comes to economy of dialogue. Again, players want a frictionless narrative; the least amount, the better. Accordingly, user interface (UI) and art teams will impose character counts on dialogue, no matter if it is voiced and subtitled; as part of an on-screen dialogue tree; or as an environmental storytelling vehicle like newspaper headlines. There is precious real estate on the screen, and every UI element has to have its own specifications so as not to distract or disrupt the others.

Games are embracing character counts more and more, so it's crucial to write with brevity. Establishing visual restrictions in a spreadsheet can help. For example, in Figure 1, I imposed a rule to shade any cells if the character count went over 70 (cell E6).

NOTES

Here, you can flag any questions you have about the line, asset ID, or category. Or if there's a mistake or an update, this column allows for the proper annotation of issues in the development cycle. Information in this column allows the other discipline specialists to be on the same page in terms of how to execute. Providing links to other documents within a drive shared by the team will allow others to click and determine how best to advise.

Notes are also an opportunity to add suggestions for the creative that have yet to be explored, especially if the dialogue is going to be performed. Casting suggestions, tone recommendations for the actor, potential alternative line rewrites, etc. help the writer see what steps need to be addressed in the recording of the talent.

PIPELINE

Typically, the narrative designer will create the spreadsheet and fill it with data, such as asset IDs, character count, and the lines (yes, once again, dialogue is data).

As touched upon earlier, once the writing is complete, the spreadsheet will be handed off to a pure designer who will input the lines and asset IDs into game. (Alternately, an audio engineer will do the same if the lines are voiced, but only after they've cleaned the data by removing unnecessary yet subtle background noise.)

Concurrently, the designer will import the data into a database for localization. That team will provide translations of the on-screen text or voice-over into several languages in subtitle form (if the dialogue is voiced) or as substitute on-screen text in a different language.

The quality assurance (QA) team will then play the game and see if there are any bugs in the narrative to assure proper implementation and/or coherence of the writing. If a line is improperly triggered, the QA team can refer to the original spreadsheet to see what needed to be launched in its place. Thereafter, the team notifies the relevant parties – pure design, audio, and/or narrative design – on what needs to be fixed.

Additionally, if the writing was properly launched, but the content itself is deficient – either through lack of coherence, typos, or lines from characters that are off-tone – the QA team will report these bugs for the narrative designer or writer to revise.

This process will continue until content is locked for the entire game, wherein there are no more opportunities to optimize. (Exceptions being title updates, but those are often specific to a new feature being launched or intended for colossal bugs that have huge downstream effects.)

The pipeline of narrative creation and implementation is a tight one. The process is very specific to the games industry. It is one that a writer is required to adopt or else he/she will struggle to be an asset to the team.

CHAPTER 5

Character and World

G REAT STORIES ARE MADE of great characters. Charisma, honor, intelligence, quirkiness, eccentricities are psychological building blocks of characters we love. Our emotional investment would not be possible without, first, a compelling central character.

THE PROTAGONIST

Players, readers, and audience members experience story through the lens of the protagonist. Also known as a hero, the protagonist is the center of all drama. They either create events that affect its plot or are subject to these events that also affect the plot. Without a protagonist, there is no journey or point of view. There is just a series of events with no cohesion or justification of plot escalation.

The protagonist is the magnet of the author's imagination. And whatever additions or subtractions the author makes to the story, they will affect the protagonist more than the other characters. The hero is the cornerstone of a story's theme, conflict, premise, and structure; how they pursue their journey and how they change at the end govern all of the above.

The protagonist doesn't have to be likeable or even honorable in a traditional sense. They just have to have their own code and be loyal to it. The lengths they go to maintain it make them compelling. Walter White from *Breaking Bad* is a morally repugnant human being. However, his sick obsession with always being right and being the smartest person in the room (as evidenced by his making the best Meth in the marketplace) compels audiences to obsess over his every move. We root for him because we cannot believe he continues to get away with murder – both literally and figuratively. Audiences are captivated by his sense of purpose.

We are also captivated by the underdog. Walter White led a disappointing life as a school teacher with a PhD, taking care of a wife and a disabled son. Diagnosed with inoperable lung cancer, Walter dedicates himself to applying his education as a chemist through the making and selling of enough crystal meth to provide for his family after his death. However, the fact that he created the most addictive drug in the market validated his sense of worth. Finally, his life as a chemist is paying off. And his skills, while underappreciated before, are beloved by countless addicts because they keep buying his drug. This is sick and twisted. But it makes sense based on how poorly his life was lead up to now. All of us can relate to being an underdog in some part of our lives – at school, at work, in relationships, in business. Walter's journey is wish fulfillment to some degree. His ability to gain wealth and validation in such a short time is something we all crave. How he got there is reprehensible; nonetheless, in fiction, audiences, players, and readers constantly yearn to escape from everyday life, even for a brief moment. We live vicariously through characters we can relate to, or – in regards to Walter White – who help us imagine how we can beat the odds like they do.

Change is also a factor in how compelling a protagonist can be. If a character does not learn from mistakes, does not adapt to challenges, or does not evolve from static situations, they become stale and one-dimensional very quickly. The genius behind *Breaking Bad* lies behind Walter White's refusal to become good. His singular focus on being the greatest meth maker in the Southwest only added more complexity to his depravity. His ability to outwit drug lords was some of the most entertaining television in the history of the medium. Walter White changed not from being bad to good, but from being bad to worse. A compelling character change does not require that they abandon who they are in order to be whom the world wants them to be. It is more compelling, in fact, if they hold true to who they are and expand on it. In the world of a story, a great character does not bend to the world; the world bends to them.

This isn't to say that you can't have a character turn from bad to good (or good to bad). A character's transformation to their polar opposite has to be seeded throughout the story and must escalate organically with every challenge the hero faces. How do they learn about themselves with every new challenge? How can they see that what they did in the past will no longer work in the future? If there are new people in their life, how do they respond to situations that feel familiar? Above all, how are they changing?

MAKING A PROTAGONIST THAT PEOPLE WILL WANT TO PLAY

When creating your main hero, you have to think about what makes them compelling and memorable. You also have to think of your player. Will they want to play your game through the lens of your hero?

You, therefore, have to ask yourself: what strengths does this hero possess? What are their weaknesses? Is there something from their backstory that they are burdened by? Have they adopted a specific purpose or mission as a result of something from their past? Do they have people close to them? If so, who are they? How did they get to where they are by the start of the game?

Once those basic questions are answered, I recommend diving deeper through a Protagonist Survey. The results lead to a rich dataset that informs how to write dialogue for a hero (or any character, for that matter) and what actions they will take in response to a story beat. Below is a sample survey. You can modify it anyway you like. What's important is identifying granular, psychological details as a foundation for rich, memorable characters (Table 3).

TABLE 3   Protagonist Survey

Which character?	Dolly
What is their role?	Dolly is the main hero/protagonist
What makes them noble?	Dolly grew up a peasant, but fought in a war that saved her village from destruction. Warriors looked up to her as their new leader
What makes them vulnerable?	Dolly has no family of her own; she was born an orphan, left for the villagers to take care of her. She finds herself often seized by moments of great isolation, even when surrounded by others; she's reluctant to trust people, until they have proven themselves. She is rigid in her views of dignity, morality, and etiquette almost to a point where she is often prematurely intolerant or quick to judge
What purpose do they have that is greater than themselves?	With no family of her own, Dolly views each citizen of her village as her family. She lives for them and will fight for them even if it leads to her own death
What is a unique strength of this character?	She can summon the dead with spells; with an amulet she found in battle, she can increase her strength tenfold; she has the courage and savvy of ten men
Why are they chosen? What makes them uniquely suited for this journey?	Upon the savage death of the village's elder statesman, Dolly will seek revenge upon those who murdered this man, her father-figure.

This survey allows a writer to hone in on what kind of hero they want to create. It also defines the character psychologically and tests whether or not the hero's personality is compelling enough to be heroic. Of course, a writer will never truly know how compelling the character is until the game, book, TV episode, or film is in the marketplace. To optimize for success, a writer must continue to ask themselves a flood of questions so that the specificity gets deeper and richer. If possible, test the traits with a focus group a few times in pre-production. The data will help indicate or solidify what makes your hero compelling.

THE ANTAGONIST

One must never forget that every good hero has to have a good villain. When defining the villain, the same initial questions have to be asked: What strengths does this villain possess? What are their weaknesses? Is there something from their backstory that they are burdened by? Have they adopted a specific purpose or mission as a result of something from their past? Do they have people close to them? If so, who are they? How did they get to where they are by the start of the game?

And most importantly, how did they become "evil?" Granted, not all antagonists are evil. They are, in their most basic sense, hindrances to the protagonist. It is the level of their being a hindrance that determines their depth of evil. Repurpose the earlier-mentioned survey (Table 3) to make your villain compelling.

But first, get to the root of who your antagonist is at a high level. There are four kinds:

- *The evil sadist.* This character is born evil (or with the seeds of it) and just wants to wreak havoc because, simply put, that's who they are. There is no higher purpose. They are driven instead by an inexplicable thirst for causing harm. He could be a lone wolf psychopath, a criminal mastermind, or a chaos maker. He usually has no regard for his own safety; however, he has an impenetrable focus and usually achieves what he aims for. Anton Chigurh from Cormac McCarthy's novel *No Country for Old Men* (also adapted to an Academy Award-winning film by the Coen Brothers) is a perfect example. The Joker from the *Batman* franchise (film, TV, comics, games, etc.) is another.

- *The obstacle.* This is someone who feels infiltrated by the protagonist and will do everything in their power to stymie the protagonist's progress. The Obstacle Villain could be either:

- Sympathetic – they are virtuous or driven to protect what they have and feel threatened by someone whose success could remove, reduce, or erode what the antagonist has. (A good example: Batman in the 2000 "Tower of Babel" story arc in the *JLA* comic series.)

- Indifferent or oblivious – This villain is extremely myopic in his/her focus in life. The hero will find it difficult to engage with them because the villain is not concerned with anything, but themselves. The personality traits range from narcissistic to cold to even good-natured. What ties these traits together is *action of omission*. In other words, what they are not doing or not being mindful of is just as harmful as an antagonist who is aggressively trying to subvert the hero. The indifferent or oblivious antagonist will cause harm as a result of:

  - Accidentally being in the protagonist's way

  - Not seeing life the same way as the protagonist does

  - Not having the same priorities, values, manners, or decency.

Del Griffith, played by John Candy in the 1987 John Hughes' comedy *Planes, Trains, and Automobiles,* is the perfect example of the oblivious antagonist. Neil Page (played by Steve Martin) is desperate to fly home and be with this family on the Tuesday before Thanksgiving, but a snowstorm forces his flight to land hundreds of miles away. A snowstorm forces his flight to land hundreds of miles away from home. From there, he inadvertently "teams up" with Del – a shower curtain ring salesman – on a reckless journey across the Midwest through various modes of transportation, each of which ultimately breaks down, making Neil's return home an increasingly unlikely prospect. Del, as it turns out, is the catalyst for nearly every single breakdown of transportation and accommodation – from stealing Neil's cab to the airport in rush hour traffic to flicking a lit cigarette in their rental car that sets it on fire to leaving his enlarged underwear in a hotel sink, with which Neil inadvertently washes his face. Del is a good-natured, kind man who can't get out of his own way. It's this obliviousness that makes him the obstacle to Neil, a tight-assed, intolerant, quintessential '80s yuppie. While Neil's frustration seems to have no limits with Del, Neil creates a bond with him as a result of Del's good nature and eventually learns that kindness and patience are two indelible traits of being a decent person.

- *The controller.* This antagonist has a rapacious thirst for money and/ or power. His goal is to amass as much of it as possible, manipulate people to help him achieve this end, and destroy those who get in his way. He could be a thief, a dictator, a greedy capitalist, a bully who uses people, a dark lord, or a cult leader. He is often charismatic and social and is a leader of people. His darkness is often the great motivator of others: while they may love him, it is their fear of him that drives their loyalty. Examples include Zachary Hale Comstock (*BioShock Infinite*), Lord Voldemort (*Harry Potter* series), Darth Vader (*Star Wars* original trilogy), and Loki (*Thor* franchise).

- *The competitor.* This type of antagonist is common in sports movies. He/she's not necessarily a bad person, but is often arrogant and maybe even better at the craft than the protagonist is. This antagonist wants to achieve the same goal as the hero does, but only one of them can obtain it. This type of character could easily be the protagonist of his/her own story if the POV were flipped. Therefore, one must look at this type of antagonist as having the same nobility as the protagonist; he/she is just a vehicle to test the protagonist to see how far they can push themselves to become the best. Examples: Iceman (*Top Gun*), Apollo Creed (*Rocky I & II*).

Unity of Opposites

No matter the type of villain you create, he/she must be fundamentally opposed to the hero in order to bring on a meaningful "unity of opposites." This is a term coined by Lajos Egri in *The Art of Dramatic Writing*. The unity of opposites assures that the sustained conflict, upon which all compelling stories are driven, is a result of deep-rooted differences between the protagonist and the antagonist whereby "compromise is impossible."* What this means is if the conflict is resolved quickly, then there is no animus between the two characters that merits a story. There has to be a vast gulf in morality or perspective of the world that drives the hero and the villain to vanquish the other. Without that intense need, there is no story, there is no interesting hero, and there is no villain worth fighting.

A Note about Hannibal Lecter

After reviewing the breakdown of villain types, one might ask, "Where's Hannibal Lecter? Sure, he might not run the Galactic Empire or attempt

---

* (Egri 1960: 123)

to relegate a mystic into an eternal dark dimension, but he tears the faces off of police officers and eats people." While those acts are cruel and sick, Hannibal Lecter was the antagonist for neither *Red Dragon* nor *The Silence of Lambs*. In fact, he was never the villain in any of the books, movies, or the *Hannibal* TV series. In the latter (as well as in the *Hannibal* and *Hannibal Rising* books), he is the protagonist … albeit an opportunistic one.

Originally, Hannibal was a supporting character in the aforementioned books and movie adaptations. Imprisoned for life for multiple cannibalistic homicides, he served as a twisted mentor and guide to FBI profiler Will Graham and later to FBI cadet Clarice Starling, each of whom was on the hunt for a different serial killer that could strike at any moment. Hannibal's past as a psychiatrist and (let's face it) psychopath provided Graham and Starling the information they needed to catch their killer before another victim was murdered. Hannibal might've slightly interfered in their investigations, but never did he derail them. Therefore, he was never a direct or meaningful obstacle to these protagonists.*

That is the key here. Even if there is a character in your story who is sick, demented, and violent, he/she poses no direct threat to your protagonist if there isn't a fundamental obstacle that cannot be corrected through compromise. Another way of looking at it: if that psychopathic character is not the main driver of the conflict in your story, he/she is not the antagonist.

ARCHETYPES AND STOCK CHARACTERS

In addition to the villain, the supporting characters will play a major part in the fiction of the game. Many times, authors rely on character archetypes to help determine who surrounds the protagonist. Archetypes are established figures that have endured for thousands of years in storytelling and are visible in movies, games, and TV shows even to this day. A foundation was set – at least in the identification of archetypes – by Carl Jung in the early 1900s.[†] Some examples and comparable contemporary characters are shown in Table 4.

---

* Now, you might think Francis Dolarhyde (*Red Dragon*) or Buffalo Bill (*The Silence of the Lambs*) weren't direct obstacles to Will Graham or Clarice Starling, respectively, mainly because the villains didn't know anyone was on their trail until the end. How could they stop a protagonist they didn't know even existed? They do qualify as antagonists, however, because they pre-emptively created obstacles for any investigator by effectively obscuring the physical details of their murders. What wasn't seen was just as obstructive as what was in plain sight. This is typical of the murder mystery and thriller genres.

† (Jung 1969: 15)

TABLE 4 Jungian Archetypes

Archetype	Role	Example(s) in Media
Wise Old Man	The person who provides knowledge and guidance to the protagonist and helps them transform into a hero.	Yoda (*Star Wars* franchise); Obi-Wan Kenobi (*Star Wars* franchise)
The Trickster	A figure who is seemingly a friend or ally, but is mischievous and untrustworthy and is responsible for an event that puts the protagonist in harm's way.	Lando Calrissian (*The Empire Strikes Back*); Little Finger (*Game of Thrones*)
The Fair Maiden	A character that represents purity and virtue; often a love interest for the protagonist; often comes from regal stock; a common target for villains as a way to hurt the protagonist. (NOTE: While this character's previous place in literature is culturally insensitive in this day and age, the role is no longer designated to young women only. Men too have assumed this role, though the numbers are still small.)	Princess Leia (*Star Wars* franchise); Kevin (*Ghostbusters* reboot)
The Nixie	A seductress or seducer who lures people (often the protagonist or a close ally) into their lair and "sucks the life out of them."[*]	Sirens (*The Odyssey*); Zora and Lora (*God of War II*); Queen of Pain (*Dota 2*)
The Mother	A figure that is helpful, loving, and wise. Or, negatively, a figure that is secretive and dark. She devours and poisons those around her.[†] This character could have both positive and negative attributes. (The controlling, manipulative mother who is overly loving to her son and nasty to others is an overused archetype, but derives from these traits.)	**Positive Connotation:** Mrs. Gump (*Forrest Gump*); Tala (*Moana*); Ramonda (*Black Panther*). **Negative Connotation:** Cersei Lannister (*Game of Thrones*); Norma Bates (*Psycho*); Marie Barone (*Everybody Loves Raymond*)
The Child	A young character with a raw sense of emotion, almost a conduit to inexplicable, even magical or otherworldly events. He (or she) is "surrounded by unknown forces and must adjust himself to them as best as he can. Owing to this chronic state of his consciousness, it is often next to impossible to find out whether he merely dreamed something or whether he really experienced it."[‡] The Child is often not believed by adults in his/her interactions with the magical or otherworldly. The Child will also separate from his/her family to explore what these forces are either to adopt a new power or enhance the power he/she already has that enabled this connection in the first place. In some cases, the child might be kidnapped by these forces.[§]	Will Byers (*Stranger Things*); Carol Anne Freeling (*Poltergeist*); Elliott (*E.T. the Extra-Terrestrial*); Cole Sear (*The Sixth Sense*)

---

[*] Ibid, page 184.

[†] Ibid, page 82.

[‡] Ibid, page 154.

[§] Ibid.

Jung codified these characters in his dissection of the collective unconscious. He believed there are figures in our dreams that are engraved in our psyche the moment we are born. These archetypes, due to their familiarity, have been cemented in myths and fairy tales and continue to endure as compelling characters in contemporary stories.

Many of these characters serve as the foundation to "stock characters," which are an expanded set of character types, each fulfilling a predictable role. Independent of Jung's findings, these characters have been collected from various different cultures over the years (some just in the past few decades; others, in the last few centuries) and have made their way into the media of other cultures due to gradual demographic inclusion. Today, with a more discerning lens, we might dismiss many of these characters as caricatures (some, offensively so), depending on the character's lack of depth and/or excessive adoption of cultural and gender stereotypes. However, there are some that have withstood the test of time and have evolved with public consciousness and good taste. To name a few:

- *The superhero* – the protagonist with extraordinary skills and strength, who faces challenges that are cataclysmic in nature and require athletic and physical abilities that go beyond the pale of the ordinary person. The superhero is often found in the adventure, sci-fi, and action genres. Yes, the typical superhero like Wonder Woman, Batman, Superman, and Spiderman is what one might instantly associate this stock character with. However, there are mere mortals that qualify as well: Indiana Jones, Lara Croft (*Tomb Raider* series), and Nathan Drake (*Uncharted* series) to name a few.

- *The supervillain* – the direct opposite of the Superhero stock character, the Supervillain is just as powerful, but with a heartless, diabolical obsession to their mission. They possess either superhuman abilities themselves or have access to exorbitant wealth, weapons, tools, and technology that can create profound devastation. They are the epitome of darkness. Examples: Lord Voldemort (*Harry Potter* franchise); Sheev Palpatine (*Star Wars* franchise); Andrew Ryan (*BioShock*).

- *Harlequin* – A lovable and loyal character, who often brings comic relief to the story, either through side cracks or clumsiness. Examples: Claptrap (*Borderlands* series); Darcy Lewis (*Thor* film series); Snarf (*Thundercats*).

- *Loyal sidekick* – A compatriot of the protagonist; loyal, dogged protector or advocate. The most trustworthy of all those who surround the protagonist. Examples: Sancho Panza (*Don Quixote*); Chewbacca (*Star Wars* series); Robin (*Batman* franchise).

Characters in games today are often a hybrid of traits taken from archetypes and stock characters. Alternatively, some characters don't even have a specific archetype associated with them. There is no requirement to do so. Archetypes and stock characters are guides to creating a rich character universe, but they are by no means a requirement to do so.

The prime objective of creating great characters is specificity. Are they specific enough in their personality DNA that when I close my eyes and hear them speak, I can distinguish their lines from the lines of others? Other important questions to ask yourself: If that character is missing, will I miss them? Or, if they are villainous, will I want to root for my protagonist more so in order to defeat them? In other words, do I care? Am I invested in this fiction? Well-written characters are often the answer.

DIALOGUE

Of course, so much of the character's psychology is revealed not only by their actions, but also by their words. Dialogue, be it performed by an actor or written on the screen, is the personality showcase of a character. How they express themselves is just as important as what they say to move the story forward.

Many books and courses on screenwriting and playwriting spend considerable time on dialogue. This is a tricky subject mainly because not all games can afford actors for voice-over or motion capture. Many times, "dialogue" is represented as on-screen text and could either represent: the voice of the game (as in narration); an NPC; or the playable hero. Additionally, I have always found it nearly impossible to instruct people on what makes good dialogue when: (a) audiences have become increasingly fractured and have different expectations that change as frequently as social media does and (b) verbal or linguistic eccentricities bring the charm of a character to the forefront while violating many of the traditional rules of tight dialogue writing. Case in point: when a skittish opera singer named Maggie is asked to mentor a rising star named Sonja, Maggie sheepishly says "Okay" and then rolls her eyes when her boss walks away. Maggie's politeness is clear – perhaps so too is her fear of saying no to her boss. The rolling of the eyes suggests she doesn't want to mentor a younger, rising star; the message is communicated succinctly. But today, you get more value with a character who stretches out the uncertainty but neither saying "no" nor saying "yes" quickly enough allowing her boss to make the decision for her.

Maggie: Well, um, you think I'm a good match for her? I dunno.
Boss: I think you'd be perfect. What do you say?
Maggie: I mean, well, I just, it's complicated. I'm kinda thinking I'm—
Boss: Excellent! I'll have her call you.

Why is this approach more common? It extends the humor, for starters. Second, it reflects how we communicate today. Very few of us, when approached with a request we don't want to do, answer resolutely. We hem and haw. What's also revealing is how Maggie's boss exerts his power. He just assumes that, by the inability to assert herself, he can get what he wants without waiting for her to answer definitively. This would not necessarily be conveyed if Maggie had responded, "Okay" and rolled her eyes.

True, some characters might be resolute, even if they are in doubt. What that character sounds like, however, will take some creative exploration. A character's personality can be extremely arbitrary, so a writer must tailor a dialogue style to it. That said, there are some universal guidelines when writing good dialogue.

Authenticity is key to every character. How a character speaks (or writes) should reveal their psychology, behavior, background (racial, ethnic, gender), upbringing, social status, and backstory. If they are hardened due to a tough childhood, then consider the traits that need to be incorporated. Are they quiet around strangers? Are they cynical when they open their mouth? If they had a happy childhood, are they always positive in tone?

Less is more. This might be odd to bring this up in light of the example above. Nevertheless, the core idea here centers on *making sure you're not writing more than is necessary.* This isn't to say the dialogue should be a few words spoken each time (unless that's who the characters truly are). It just means there is no need to overwrite a character. Delete excess lines that express the same sentiment.

Lines need vitality. Dialogue can often be flat if there isn't an undercurrent of energy behind the character. When you write the lines, recite them out loud. Will the lines spark a good performance from the actor? Or, if just text on screen, are the lines something players will want to recite out loud to themselves?

Distinction is necessary. Do not write universal dialogue, even if the lines crackle. Make sure each character has their own distinct voice. Make the lines alive by giving the characters a signature way of expressing themselves.

Power status has a profound impact on a character's psychology. This might seem obvious to most, but you'd be surprised to see how often power status has no impact on a character's dialogue in games. It clearly goes beyond the easy shorthand of ending or beginning the dialogue with the title of a character (e.g., "Yes, Sergeant."; "At your service, My Lord."). As Shakespeare taught us in *Macbeth*, the King might rule Scotland, but the Queen rules the King; thus, a title does not always equate power. What's more important is the *psychological power* one character has over another. *Interpersonal status is a massive influencer of dialogue.* For instance, is a father afraid of his daughter because she has run away from home before and the father wants to prevent a recurrence? If so, his dialogue will be obsequious, overly accommodating, maybe even timid. Is an assassin afraid of no one? If so, then her dialogue could be indifferent, almost without affect. Or perhaps she takes pride in her skill and her lack of attachments and is, therefore, overly brash when she talks to a new client. What about two mercenaries who are unwilling to cede control to one another and are equally stubborn in how to infiltrate a terrorist safe house? If so, then their dialogue will be contentious, maybe even playful at times. Power status may not necessarily be uniform from one character to the next. Perhaps one of those mercenaries is also the same father who is afraid of his daughter. Certainly, the mercenary will not talk to her as he does to his partner.

Before the writer identifies the power status among his/her characters, it's important he/she determines what drives the characters and what the potential emotional obstacles are. Otherwise, it will be hard to convey a power dynamic and could render the dialogue flat and uninteresting.

Understand subtext. Subtext is the unspoken dialogue between characters in a scene. In the example of Maggie the opera singer, the subtext on the most superficial level was her aversion to taking on an apprentice. But why? Is Maggie in the last years of her career and does not want to compete with someone who could take her job? Was she once a rising star and was traumatized by a previous mentor and, therefore, does not want to re-enact that? Why didn't she push back on her boss? Is it fear of losing her job? Is he in a bad place in his life and she couldn't bring herself to hurting his feelings? The various unrealized feelings of a character will influence not only what they say, but more importantly *what they don't say*. This creates a deep psychological foundation of our characters and, therefore, makes them more interesting.

In violating the subtext rule, there is little to discover about the characters we create. This brings to mind the necessary cliché: "show, not tell." Allow the behavior and actions of the characters to reveal what's happening in the plot and in their emotional journey. It's not interesting for Maggie to say to her boss, "I hate you." Dumping a laxative in his coffee and feigning interest in helping him find the bathroom are more revealing of Maggie's psychological makeup. They're also more entertaining.

Sometimes, it's unavoidable for a character to talk "on the nose" or just say what they're feeling outright, especially when we need to convey a specific gameplay mechanic, like for tutorials. These introductory gameplay "how to's" are almost always subtext-free because their purpose is to arm the player with key information on how to use the controller and play the game. In other circumstances, however, subtext is revealed when the dramatic moment is earned. Will Maggie reach her tipping point with her boss? After months of mentoring the young ingenue, Maggie is let go from the opera. Under those circumstances, Maggie's confronting her boss is justified. It will allow her to unload on him and reveal past resentments in order to achieve closure to a frustrating relationship. (Aristotle referred to this as *catharsis*.) To get here, the character must go through a series of mental anguish and professional challenges, during which time the subtext of Maggie's dialogue becomes more multi-dimensional and complex.

Dialogue is elusive in the gaming world, mainly because casting is usually a last-minute addition. Writing for specific actors, therefore, is not recommended.* Dialogue is elusive also because performers aren't usually acting off of one another. They are isolated in a sound booth, reciting lines usually out of context. Also, because of their massive expanse, games don't always have a singular script. Lines can be recited as combat chatter or for ambient authenticity, or as an in-game dialogue moment to help move the gameplay along. These are often presented on-screen in a spreadsheet or as hard copies … of spreadsheets. Cut scenes are often the exception, but only in presentation. An actor will be presented with a script, but will have no one to act off of, except for the voice director … who is not in the recording booth with the actor.

---

* Unless, of course, the game is an already established franchise with confirmed actors or you have actors in mind as north star "comparables" to guide casting.

Because of these challenges, a narrative designer or game writer will need to supplement the script with a bullet-proof tone document and character bio to help inform the actor's performance. There will be off-the-cuff feedback during the recording sessions, so script changes will happen on the fly.

ESTABLISH WORLDS AND OTHER SIGNATURE ELEMENTS

Successful games have characters, worlds, and moments that are brandable and ownable. More specifically, a game's unique elements must be front and center and must be significant enough to differentiate it from the competition. Without these unique elements, the game will fail to capture consumers.

These differentiators are critical because they go beyond the game experience. In print ads and reviews, memorable images will capture cool-looking vehicles or a savage confrontation between two dynamic, vivid characters. These still images will also be on the front and back of the game package or as a thumbnail image in a digital store (via PlayStation Network, Xbox Live, Steam, App store, etc.). Gameplay clips also have their impact on creating ownable differentiation.

These images speak to something larger than a manipulation in marketing. It's about creating memorable, sticky characters and worlds that provide the game with the possibility of going beyond its original medium. Could I experience another journey of Nathan Drake in, say, an *Unchartered* movie? I will delve into this further in the transmedia section of this book, but it's important to bring up this topic up now because, next to structure, creating ownable worlds and characters is the most important part of a narrative designer's job. Gameplay can thrive on its own by tapping into a gamer's dopamine pleasure centers. But games are a competitive business. Without a vibrant world and memorable characters that players will want to play, they will buy the competitor's product over yours, plain and simple.

Narrative may not be the main selling point for most games. But games that do not offer narrative will struggle to differentiate themselves in the marketplace.

Think of a world as a character. Like a good character, a compelling world should have distinct, memorable features that invoke emotion in players – comfort, distrust, mystery, menace, resolve, etc. In asking yourself what makes a world distinct, you will wind up writing a backstory that is not unlike those of your characters. Set up a profile of this world, as you would a character. Here are some prompts to help you define the world you're trying to build (Table 5).

TABLE 5   World-as-Character Survey

What's the name of this world?	Piedmont
Where is it?	A town somewhere in New England; state unknown
How many people live there?	508. It's rural
What kind of people live there?	60% is made up of Army veterans; most are out of work and rely on the bottle to get through the day; 20% is Native American, as there's a reservation nearby and a casino not far away; the remaining 20% of Piedmont is a biker gang, who sells illegal firearms to subsidize the empire of their brotherhood
Name an historical event that happened there in the past 20 years.	A senator was killed in a mysterious car accident that some have suggested was engineered by the biker gang out of revenge for his supporting new Federal funding to the ATF (American Tobacco and Firearms)
What's the climate of this world?	Long winters. It snows starting in early October and ends in early May. The town experiences subzero temperatures during this time, along with heavy snowfall and limited hours of light. The summers are extremely humid. Moderate temperatures in May and September
What's the world look like?	Working class town with high unemployment. Biggest employers are the casino 10 miles away and the ValleyMart, a huge discount department store. Lots of trailer parks. Houses have acres of space between one another. The woods are thick, filled with heavy streams but barren trees. Lots of RVs on abandoned streets. People do not pick up after themselves. It's a third world town inside of a first world country
How do the people in the neighboring worlds feel about it?	No respect for Piedmont. As far others can tell, this is a barren wasteland. If you're not drowning your sorrows at the local saloon, you're tattooing your flesh to celebrate your gang
Who runs this world?	Derrick Ambrose, the leader of the Devil Spawn Biker gang. He is the most feared man in the state, but as long as you keep to yourself, you won't have any trouble
How is this world run?	Gangland rules. No snitches, no stiches. As long as you let the Devil Spawn gang do as they please, you'll be fine. But if you cross them, your days are numbered
Are there any rivalries in this world?	Rival gangs occasionally drive through here, but at great risk. Recently, the Mafia set up shop in order to invest in the nearby casino
Are there any intruders or threats to this world?	The Mafia and undercover ATF agents, who track the activities of the gang
What's the most recent event that set the world into chaos?	The sister of an Army vet was killed at a local bar. Her boyfriend, a gang member of the Devil Spawn, fled the town

(Continued)

TABLE 5 (CONTINUED)   World-as-Character Survey

Is the status quo of this world being threatened? If so, how?	Yes. The Army vet is investigating what happened. Denied by the police because they don't want to cross the Devil Spawn, the Army vet has taken to arms to exact revenge on this gang, even joining forces with the Mafia to take them down
Is there an event that the world is preparing for or responding to?	A massive snowstorm has cut the power supply off to the town. Everyone is living without electricity for the indefinite future. The roads are too dangerous to travel on
Will this world survive in five years?	No. It is on the verge of moral collapse if the gang cannot rise from the cover up of the death of the Army vet's sister. Alternatively, the Mafia might take it over if they see a town in turmoil with crumbling leadership

When describing the world, one cannot help but dig into its political nature. This is what makes world building a fun endeavor. Worlds need to be filled by living entities. Each of those entities has an agenda. Entities will go at war when agendas clash. World building is about creating a tension-filled showcase for your characters.

Now, it's likely you will need to describe in detail the physical nature of the world, where the different inhabitants live, and its climactic elements. While I only touched upon these briefly, I find that this exercise is less about storytelling than it is about creating a blueprint from which artists and designers build. Writers and narrative designers can spend too much time getting into the granular details of describing the visual nature of the world, as if they were a geologist writing down the various physical properties of a newly discovered rock. I do not find this to be a good use of a writer's time. While there is value in providing enough physical details to help artists do their job, the storyteller should look at world building as an opportunity to inform compelling characters, introduce potential conflicts, and create a rich tapestry that influences how the lore of the intellectual property unfolds over time.

CHAPTER 6

Structure

WHAT IS STRUCTURE AND WHY IS IT IMPORTANT?

Dramatic structure is the sequence of story-driven events that provides a natural escalation to a protagonist's journey. Structure gives a story its shape, or more specifically, a coherent organization of moments that provide the maximum entertainment, character development, and necessary setbacks that make subsequent resolutions enjoyable and meaningful.

A protagonist's journey is not fulfilling if there are no obstacles to overcome. In fact, a protagonist becomes more admirable and more heroic with every escalating challenge that they overcome. The greater the challenge, the greater the effort. The more successful the effort, the greater the heroism. The greater the heroism, the greater the hero.

Structure is just as important as character. In fact, structure is the one element of storytelling that is the least controversial, simply because there is a natural logic to a sequence of events that, if violated, would render a story incomprehensible. Moreover, ignoring obstacles, their escalation, and resolution would render a story dull, stale, and stagnant.

WHERE GAMES FAIL

Structure is oftentimes given the backseat treatment because of the numerous concessions that writers have to make for gameplay, development rescoping, and budget pressures. But it is also the case that poor precedent was set in the early days of games. Why? Many of the early days of narrative were not written by writers, but more so by game designers who had little-to-no knowledge of story structure or character development.

(Thankfully, the effort to uproot this precedent – and basically destroy it – is ongoing.)

MAIN STRUCTURAL BEATS

When I am brought on a new project, I make sure to have the creative director, lead designer, producer, and others in a single room, where we hash out the big moments of the game's story. Usually, the team will already have a set of "non-negotiables," that is, required moments that provide the biggest impact on gameplay and on the hero's journey. I then work with them to figure out the main story beats in between these key gameplay moments. From there, we work toward establishing a structure and a natural escalation of events.

Over the years, I have evaluated the following story concepts from some of the best dramatists and story theorists in the field. Not one theorist offers a clean set of story milestones that work perfectly for games. Therefore, I have cherry picked story milestones from these various thinkers and have added my own to the following list. I can attest to their effectiveness, as I have applied this combination of milestones to numerous games I've worked on. Other games might apply the same structural milestones, though their terminology might vary from studio to studio.

Act 1

Inciting Incident – the first significant moment in the story that redefines that *status quo* of the world of the protagonist. This moment has a downstream effect that impacts everything in that world and eventually forces the protagonist to take an action that officially sets the story in motion.

Introduction to Protagonist's Purpose – a protagonist might be morally unscrupulous, pure-of-heart, unimposing, enterprising, or quiet. What is important is determining clearly and upfront what drives them. This is the most important building block of a protagonist's personality DNA. A great example of this is in the first episode of *Breaking Bad*. After his diagnosis of terminal cancer, Walter White makes a clear-cut decision to collaborate with a former student to make and distribute crystal meth. His goal (at least at first) is to generate over $900,000 so that, after his death, his wife, disabled son, and unborn child will have enough money to survive on their own.

Fans of the show will realize later on that Walter White's ambition does not end there. His eyes eventually set on becoming the biggest drug kingpin in the Southwest. But, it takes a long while for us to get there. In the meantime, our sympathies are with a dying Walter White in his selfless crusade to make and sell drugs. The goal is very clear as are his priorities. We, as viewers, make the decision to go along with him. Conversely, if the goals are not clear from the outset, it's very difficult to get bought in on the hero's journey when we don't know what he/she is committed to.

Poorly written heroes do not have defined goals.

Refuse the Call – the moment where the protagonist is offered an opportunity to do something profound and significant, but declines because they feel there is no path to success at that moment, mainly due to a lack of courage or feasibility.

Situation Worsens – the life of the protagonist, after refusing the call, worsens. Either the *status quo* is threatened, a rival emerges, or the hero's sensibilities are offended. No matter the scenario, the protagonist must feel as if life is untenable or unacceptable and reconsiders their act of refusing the call. Perhaps if they re-answer it, they will reverse their current negative trend in life.

Accept the Call – after the situation for our hero or his loved ones worsens, the hero realizes they cannot accept things as they are. They must commit to taking action and putting themselves in harm's way to save those in danger.

If the story is not a violent one, then the comparable scenario to harm's way could be anything that puts the protagonist outside of their comfort zone. They are in a new role, for example, that challenges them in ways they did not expect. Proving that they can handle this role will determine their heroism. But, the path forward cannot occur unless the protagonist accepts the new role.

Point of No Return – the protagonist has succeeded in performing their first act of heroism. In doing so, they are too committed (and inextricably linked) to the mission that they cannot turn back.

Act 2

Adjustment to New World – on their journey to accomplishing the mission, they will need to adjust to their new surroundings. This should not be easy for the hero, as every hardship – big or small – makes the hero more adaptable, more honorable, and stronger.

Escalating Burdens – this new world involves new hardships and conflicts that increase in complexity and intensity the further the protagonist travels. Once again, every new challenge – big or small – is an opportunity for the protagonist to become better at (1) what they do as a practitioner of their craft and (2) who they are as a thinking, feeling person.

Escalating burdens is shorthand for new conflicts that arise and threaten our hero's existence. They can be physical challenges (climbing a mountain; crossing a sea; etc.) or emotional ones (a femme fatale leaves the hero's house with the stolen money; an angry partner feels betrayed by a hero and leaves the mission). They often involve their own microstories, especially if the medium is episodic. If the medium is structured like a 3-act structure (which most films and games are), then escalating burdens will take up most of Act 2. They are a series of challenges that threatens the hero continually while increasing in danger. Escalating burdens drive the plot forward. They are the logistics of a story and are often a different class from larger narrative milestones.

In other words, escalating burdens are often the "what happens next" instances of story.

Exposure of Weakness – every good story has a moment where the hero's momentum stops, and the audiences (or players) are forced to re-evaluate the journey and the protagonist. This is the low point of the story. But, the buildup to the low point is essential; the hero cannot suddenly lose everything and expect the audience to feel something. There has to be a sense of doubt instilled in the viewer long before the low point happens. Here, you can plant the seeds. These momentary weaknesses might seem like nothing, especially if the hero continues to excel. But once a major event occurs wherein the hero's weakness leads to the destruction of a village, for example, the perception of the hero *as a hero* is in grave doubt. Sure, a weakness for wine means nothing if the hero wakes up with a hangover and enters the dark forest the next day. There was nothing at stake; no meaningful consequences of their actions.

If, however, they chose to drink wine that night and got too sloshed to run to the village and stave off a massacre from marauders, such a weakness is unforgivable, but possibly redemptive.

Loss of Trust – once the weakness is exposed for what it is, the protagonist will lose the trust of those around him and of the audience (or players). Exposure of Weakness and Loss of Trust are complementary and symbiotically connected; you cannot have one without the other. Loss of trust should be the emotional consequences of the low point, whereas exposure of weakness is the logistical consequence.

Midpoint/Low Point – this is the story beat where – coupled with Exposure of Weakness and Loss of Trust – the protagonist's fortunes are reversed. A single act has led to a full stop to the hero's progress and to the deprivation of something important, e.g., the decimation of a village they were meant to protect; an abduction of a loved one; the destruction of a weapon; the death of a close friend, loved one, or relative. Whatever the event, the hero should feel their own sense of doubt. Is finishing the mission even possible? Will they survive? Will the people that mean the most to the hero survive or permanently lose faith in him/her? This is a moment of great despair and the most necessary story beat in terms of escalation. While everything is rising and the hero rises with it, a drop as severe as this one truly tests the hero. How they adapt to this low moment will determine if they are a hero and, if so, will define what kind of hero they are.

The most effective of low points happens as a result of a hero making a choice they shouldn't have. Opting to drink wine at the local tavern over guarding your village is a perfect example. The choice reveals a psychology about the hero that will need to be planted earlier. The hero's drinking could either be a sign of an addiction or a casual arrogance where they believe everything's good if there are no signs of danger in sight. Neither scenario makes a hero. In a later story beat, the hero should learn from that weakness and work twice as hard to remedy their mistake or flaw while delivering on their most heroic effort yet.

In the Belly of Jonah's whale – after the low point, the hero moves forward but in a fog (either mentally or physically). Their pace is slower and there is great confusion as to where they need to go next. Usually, it is a moment of stagnation. It is akin to being *in utero*, where the hero is floating powerlessly without direction.

There is uncertainty in this stage, which may involve physical threats to one's life or mental anguish where one doubts themselves. To survive this moment is to re-emerge from it a new hero, better than before.

This concept was identified by the philosopher Joseph Campbell with regard to the Biblical parable of Jonah and the whale. Jonah, in defying God's orders to preach to the people of Nineveh, headed on a boat to Tarsish where he was soon caught up in a great storm. The men on the boat blamed Jonah for the storm, for it was clearly a result of God's wrath, and threw him overboard. Jonah was then swallowed by a whale, where he then repented and pleaded to God to be spared. At last, he got "spit up" by the whale on the shores of Nineveh, where Jonah visited its wicked citizens and preached the word of God.

As Joseph Campbell points out:

> The conscious personality here has come in touch with a charge
> of unconscious energy which it is unable to handle and must now

suffer all the trails and revelations of a terrifying night sea journey, while learning how to come to terms with this power of the dark and emerge, at last, to a new way of life.*

This story beat is about the hero's facing their innermost demons and slaying them only to be reborn braver and stronger.

Act 3

Redemption Path Begins – once the protagonist has survived the grueling stasis inside the belly of Jonah's whale, they emerge as a new hero, repurposed or rededicated to achieving their initial goal. They have adopted a new zealotry with a tacit code: "I will achieve my goal by any means necessary." Their motivation brings them to the next level of hero status. Where once they were a timid protagonist who rose to the occasion when needed, they are now proactive, single-minded, intense, and strong willed. They are willing to die for their cause. This story beat can straddle between the end of the second act or the beginning of the third.

Ticking Time Bomb Introduced – our new hero will face an overwhelming obstacle like no other. While they have emerged as a better warrior as a result of prevailing over Jonah's whale, the difficulty in achieving their initial goal amplifies. This is a must; otherwise, the story would run stale quickly if an omnipotent hero has an easy path ahead. The figurative ticking time bomb is either a rapid escalation of the main villain's goals or an introduction of a new threat to vanquish the protagonist or those he/she holds dear.

Escalating Burdens Intensify – the ticking time bomb isn't the only obstacle the hero must face in Act 3. They will encounter numerous warriors, environmental threats, and interpersonal struggles that exacerbate the tension created by the ticking time bomb. These burdens keep getting in the hero's way, reducing the odds of stopping the ticking time bomb from "blowing up." Escalating burdens increase suspense by compelling the player or audience to ask themselves, "Will the hero make it in time to stop the bomb?"

Obligatory Scene/Climax – once the hero has resolved all the escalating burdens and is on the verge of stopping the ticking time bomb, they must face the antagonist. This is the final showdown between good vs. evil, also known as the obligatory scene. In video games, these scenes are known as

---

* (Campbell 1988: 180–181)

"Boss Battles"; however, every game has numerous boss battles, but ultimately lead to a final one. Nonetheless, the principle behind it is the same: each objective or mission leads up to an ultimate confrontation before a player can move forward. Other media do not have that kind of creative mandate. It's important, still, to designate the final boss battle as the obligatory scene, so that the dramatic tension can be properly built beforehand.

This story beat isn't just important from a logistical sense (defeating the villain in order to stop the bomb); it's also important from a moral sense. Evil should not prevail. Every protagonist knows this implicitly; therefore, defeating the villain is a moral imperative. This confrontation is also the climax of the story, aka, its most important moment. It's what your entire story is intended to lead to. One can determine the depth of its importance by identifying what would happen if the hero lost (case in point: instant destruction of the community they were dedicated to saving). The stakes cannot get any higher than this moment.

Reversal – when analyzing Athenian drama, Aristotle identified a key moment in every play where the status of the protagonist shifted, either from good to bad, bad to good, or from any position or perspective to its opposite. This is known as a reversal.* This story beat has endured for thousands of years and finds its way in games, books, and movies today. In the last 50 years, no film has had a better reversal than in *Godfather II* (1974). When Kay, the wife of the powerful crime boss Michael Corleone, reveals to him that the baby she lost in pregnancy was not due to a miscarriage, as originally thought, but to an abortion, Michael (the hero) is instantly shattered. No matter what power he could wield as a Mafia boss, what was important to him, above everything else, was family. His reversal went from powerful to powerless within seconds.

Recognition – in response to the reversal, Aristotle observed that the protagonist must have a moment where they must switch from "ignorance to knowledge"† in their relationship to the world around them. In Michael Corleone's case, his true understanding behind the loss of Kay's baby forced him to see he was not as powerful as he thought. He was the most feared leader in organized crime. But as a man, his rapacious desire for power pushed his wife away to such a point where she aborted their child so that future generations of Corleones could never wreak havoc on this earth. As a result of this revelation, he lashed out at Kay – both physically

---

* (Aristotle n.d.: 18)
† Ibid, pages 18–19.

and verbally. This uncharacteristic move derived from Michael's recognition of his failure as a husband and man. But that recognition did not stop him from continuing his heartless journey; instead he doubles down on it and commits the most heinous of crimes: the killing of his brother Fredo, as a result of an unrelated double-cross. It is not necessary for the hero to change once they've achieved recognition. What is necessary, however, is that they are *given the opportunity to change*. Whatever action they take then – be it to change or to stay the course – will define the type of protagonist they are.

Resolution of the Bomb – just because your hero has defeated the antagonist doesn't mean the ticking time bomb has stopped at the same time. There's still work to be done. And fast. The bomb continues to tick as a lingering, imminent threat. If the hero stops to take a breath after defeating the villain, it's too late. The bomb will go off, leading to utter devastation. The hero at this point has nothing to prove. They aren't looking for a pat on the back or payment for services rendered. Their next move is a reflexive, visceral response to save the day … in mere seconds. Taking action is less about the hero's valor or duty than it is about the hero's innate sense of selflessness. It's the community the hero's been fighting for, not the desire to become a hero. But by saving the community, the hero truly becomes a hero.

Denouement – when the ticking time bomb has been resolved, the hero and his/her community can relax. Everyone will take the next steps to achieve a new *status quo*. We're all familiar with the common tropes. The hero and a love interest kiss. The community celebrates the hero. People take precautions to prevent the rise of the villain. All of these events make up the denouement: the collective sigh of relief paired with the early signs of life returning to normal. Not all stories have a denouement. Some will end with a sense of unease, *ala* the villain rises from the ashes to signal a sequel or the hero is compromised irrevocably. The 1970s conspiracy thrillers – for example, *The Parallax View* or *Three Days of the Condor* – exemplify this type of ending.

PLEASE NOTE: Don't kill yourself trying to get the precise order of these milestones in place. The point is to be aware of their general proximity. The sequence will be dictated by the organic development of your story.

DRAMATIC ESCALATION WARNINGS

The goal of these milestones is to build a strong, meaningful, and believable escalation of the protagonist's journey. They are like coordinates for the story, such as: when the character is introduced to the challenge; or when the character must face off against the villain. These coordinates provide navigational guidance on how to craft the forward momentum of a story.

While I am stickler for taut structure, I cannot expect other writers and narrative designers to be the same way. What is important – in fact, what is necessary – is dramatic escalation. Is the story steadily moving upward in terms of the stakes of the hero and the challenges he/she will face? Escalation is the baseline; without that, there is no story.

In games, however, narrative escalation can be undermined through gameplay. This can happen in a few ways.

Premature Character Introduction

People love bad guys. In games, people love killing bad guys. Bad guys often appear early on as a way to foreshadow more bad things to come. But when the bad guy appears semi-frequently, it often ruins the moment when the player has to face off against them in a final obligatory scene (aka final Boss Battle). The powers of the bad guys are not surprising as you've already been exposed to them prior to the final confrontation. Moreover, if you meet a rogue's gallery of cooler characters in between every appearance of said bad guy, it's hard to avoid disappointment when the final boss battle arrives.

The same goes for sports games. If the cover athlete of the game happens to be one of the best in the league but not *the* best, the final match-up in a linear tutorial (that is, an in-depth pregame experience to teach you basic mechanics) will be problematic. There will be a clear logical disconnect if, for instance, you face off against better-in-reality players before the cover athlete.* True, the game might be tuned or programmed where the difficulty increases from one player to the next. So, by the time you face off against the (lesser-in-reality) cover athlete, you might not notice the disparity between reality and fantasy because you're struggling to keep up. Nevertheless, it's clumsy storytelling.

---

* For example, you are a Major League baseball pitcher who has to face off against several historical Yankee legends. Your first batter is Mickey Mantle and then Babe Ruth. To strike out the side, you have to face this year's cover athlete: Don Mattingly. Now, Don Mattingly was very good from 1984–1989 and even won an MVP in 1985. But he was never on the level of Mantle or Ruth. Sports games do this often, mainly because nabbing a cover athlete is hard; studios are lucky to get a star every year. Also, because cover athletes change every year to match the annual publishing cadence of a sports title, game companies will never have the upcoming season's top star on the cover consistently, year after year.

Long Missions with No Narrative Interspersed

This is the most common obstacle in game narrative. How can you expect players to remember the details of the story when there is so much gameplay disruption in between beats? Some solutions involve in-game dialogue, where characters talk to you as you traverse an environment. Much of that dialogue is clumsy exposition, as it serves to inform players of mission progress, potential foreshadowing moments, information about the world, and loose (very loose) character development.

Nevertheless, *The Last of Us* (which I will delve into later) is extremely successful in this effort. Its ambient dialogue is varied and rich with mystery that slowly reveals the status of the world. It also enhances the tone of every dramatic situation in the game (i.e., intense when danger approaches; uncertain during suspicious quietude). Enhancing tone is the key solution to this narrative problem of long missions. *The Last of Us* makes the most out of every opportunity to tell story. Take, for instance, the situation where the game's protagonists Joel and Ellie stealthily travel from one abandoned building to the next to escape a quarantine zone. They will elude a tyrannical paramilitary force who are killing rebels on the streets. While that player might not absorb every line of dialogue that is spoken by these NPCs several yards away, he/she will absorb what's going on gradually as varied dialogue expresses and reinforces lore and tonal continuity over time. As a player, not only do I know what I'm doing long term and short term, but I'm also engrossed in my current mission because the dialogue reflects (or even shapes) how I feel. Most games do not vary their NPC ambient dialogue. It is often uniform and is more about imminent tasks ("Kill them!" or "Take cover!") than it is about revealing details of the world in an organic way or about supporting the tone of the scene.

Once again: Writers cannot force people to stop playing and absorb every narrative detail. Instead, like music and great graphics, the narrative must be an enhancement to the immersion of the gaming experience.

Arbitrary Bells and Whistles

Designers love creating cool features, but oftentimes these new features do not have narrative justification. These moments are there to enhance the player's fun, but can be completely irrelevant to the narrative. Yet, because these moments are addictive and fun to play, narrative designers have to justify their existence through story. While the length and frequency of typical gameplay moments can drown out a game's narrative, irrelevant bells and whistles can compound narrative's never-ending fight for prominence.

To solve these issues is to be in a constant state of awareness of the game's development. If there are additions that undermine the story, you must let the team know as soon as possible. If this new course can't be reversed, you must revise what is already written, not necessarily to make the story better, but to assure its coherence.

DIFFERENT LENGTHS OF THE ACTS

The 3-act structure is a tried-and-true narrative model for most console games.* Due to the emphasis of gameplay, quick intros and outros are strongly preferred. Act 1 – which is often 30 minutes in a 2-hour film – provides set-up for a game. A player will ask themselves – *What's the world I'll be playing in, what's at stake, what kind of character am I, who are my enemies?* The act ends with a huge complication that thrusts our hero onto an uncertain path where they will face one dangerous mission after another. Sounds similar to film, yes. But the difference in games is – for an 8-hour-plus experience – Act 1 can be as short as 15 minutes. All of the elements I just described are revealed at a rapid pace in order to get the players' fingers moving on the sticks (aka controller) as quickly as possible.

Act 2 is the vast majority of the gaming experience. Ranging from 6 to 40 hours, Act 2 is where the player faces difficult, yet visually stimulating challenges successively. Bits of narrative are revealed along the way, but can get lost in a morass of grinding activities. The key here is to provide consistent content that is revealed in short bites that often repeats or restates itself. This is to reinforce crucial narrative information that can get overshadowed and lost by tremendous volume of gameplay moments.

A steady stream of short narrative encounters is the best way to create a frictionless narrative that players will remember. The narrative vehicles to deliver and repeat this information do not have to be the same. A collected item that a player reads can introduce a plot point; an in-game dialogue moment with an NPC who walks with you to a location can reinforce the info you read in the collected item; and a dialogue tree conversation with an NPC can drive home the information you originally read in the collected item and can take it one step further by revealing crucial character information.

---

* Episodic games have their own structure. The structure of RPGs, for example, resembles that of a soap opera or melodrama. The Telltale Games portfolio mirrored the structure of a mini-series or a six-episode season, popularized by the British TV model.

TABLE 6 Basic Minimum Story Milestones for Act 3

Story Beat	Structural Milestone
The player is thrust into a new threat that is time sensitive with devastating effects	Ticking Time Bomb introduced
They then have to save someone or something as obstacles from the new threat get in the way	Escalating burdens
They face off against the main villain	Obligatory Scene/Climax
They might risk the safety of the person they are saving if they do not defeat the villain	Reversal
Upon defeat of the villain and the saving of the person, place, or thing …	Resolution of ticking time bomb
…. the hero has achieved a greater understanding of who they are	Recognition
The hero is loved by those he/she saved	Denouement
The hero walks off into the sunset	Denouement (cont'd)
But a rising threat emerges, foreshadowing danger ahead in a potential sequel	Sequel Hook (not required)

This can continue throughout all of Act 2 up until Act 3, which must end on a high note, both in gameplay and in story. Will the protagonist defeat the villain in the most dangerous of circumstances? This obligatory scene must be the culmination of art, gameplay, sound, programming, and every other discipline in game development. It must give players their biggest thrill after days of playing nothing but your game.

There isn't a lot of narrative in Act 3, but what's left packs a wallop. The following examples are a bit overly simplistic and paint game narrative resolution into an unfairly limited box. Nonetheless, they indicate clearly how each of these plot points corresponds to timeless story milestones in a typical Act 3 (Table 6).

From a narrative standpoint, these story beats happen quickly and are closely tied to gameplay. And if gameplay is escalating properly, its integration with narrative should reach its most symbiotic state in Act 3. One could argue that there is a natural order of events when it comes to resolving the end of a story. There is always an extreme escalation, a threat of total destruction, a confrontation, and a resolution of that confrontation (hero wins or hero loses). Games do this very well. If you've done your job well at seeding the proper narrative beats before Act 3, then allow the final story events to take their natural course. Those events, in themselves, have a natural escalation and structure.

CHAPTER 7

Meaningful Choice, Branching Narrative, and Downstream Effects

THE CONCEPT OF MEANINGFUL choice is critical in game narrative. It is one of the few times that narrative is a proactive force (as opposed to a reactive one) on gameplay.

Meaningful choice is the result of an interactive dialogue exchange between the player and the non-playable character (NPC). The interactive exchange allows the development team to provide necessary context and story while giving the player immediate incentives once they complete a dialogue exchange. Such incentives include experience points, gear to brag about to your friends, and/or tools or weapons that enhance the player's abilities (for example, a sword if it's a medieval role-playing game (RPG) or a type of sneaker if it's a sports game).

Good narrative design will make sure that a player is given more than just a sword at the end of an exchange. Good narrative design will make sure that, no matter the choices you are given in a dialogue exchange, either option will provide you with sufficient differentiated content to encourage replayability. These dialogue exchanges can create branching narrative, which is, in part, a methodology of storytelling that centers on a player's ability to make choices in the game that directly impact the outcome of the story. In a non-branching narrative (aka linear story), the outcome is proscribed and immutable. In a branching narrative, however, the outcome could have numerous endings and numerous paths to reach these endings. Branching narrative is often compared to a "Choose Your Own Adventure" book: strategic moments in the narrative (also known as decision points) encourage a player to choose one of many paths to continue the story. In games, branching narrative is most common in RPGs. Whatever the player chooses will eventually lead to further decision points that will offer, yet again, more choices. As a result of the multiplicity of choices, the player has reached a unique ending that is markedly different than numerous other endings that resulted from various routes that could have been chosen in substitution. Each ending, no matter how different, starts from the same, singular point. The first choice a player makes will set the course for a series of downstream effects that will lead to a completely different adventure from one path to the next.

This is called branching narrative because, during the story architecture of these decision points, the visual representation of "what ifs" (as in, what if you chose Choice #2 vs. Choice #3) adds up to what looks like countless branches in a large tree. In the pages that follow, I map out what a branching dialogue looks like.

But first, let's say an NPC approaches you at a gate. You cannot pass unless you engage him in a conversation. After every line of dialogue, you will have three choices of responses. Depending on your response, the NPC can continue the dialogue directly addressing the tone that you set and/or deprive you of or provide you with a new clue or opportunity to help you continue on your path. For this exercise, I have added notations next to every choice (e.g., 1a, 1b, 1c, etc.). There is no deep pattern or methodology behind them. In fact, they are omitted from the visual branching diagram I have provided later on. The notations are strictly used for clarity of this discussion. Let's start:

NPC: How are you today?

- *Choice #1a: Great. How are you?*
- *Choice #2a: Terrible. My best friend just died of scurvy.*
- *Choice #3a: Shut up and get out of my way.*

Player selects Choice #3a. Then –

NPC: Hey, that's no way to treat a stranger! Apologize now or I will impale you with my dagger.

- *Choice #1b: Methinks I drank too much mead last night. My deepest apologies.*

- *Choice #2b: You're too stupid to deserve an apology. Now, move!*
- *Choice #3b: Neither option will suffice. I shall leave you to your gatekeeping. Cheers!*

Here, Choice #1b leads the player to a new path with no struggle or threat of death, thus moving the narrative along quickly without incident. The subsequent dialogue and story beats will default to the safest path forward. Choice #2b will likely lead to a physical encounter where the player will either win and survive or lose and die. If he/she wins, a strong narrative designer would assure that the subsequent conversations will have a defensive tone from the NPCs, and likely, more conflict from other NPCs who will want to avenge the death of their friend, the gatekeeper. This choice is important because it defines the player's attitude and tone that will be adopted in every exchange thereafter. It has a clear downstream effect.

On the other hand, if the player chose Choice #3b, the player will return to where he/she was before but will not be able to progress without taking the amiable, default path (Choice #1b) or the dangerous, hostile path (Choice #2b). Choice #3b, therefore, is the weakest of the choices because it forces the player to retry the unchosen options to move forward without offering any new information about plot or character. Strong narrative branching must allow every choice to: (a) lead to different outcomes; (b) move the plot forward; (c) or provide more information about the character or world that is not obvious.

A better Choice #3b could have been: "*That dagger of yours? It looks familiar. Was that given to you by Johan Lankersheim?*" The response –

NPC: Why, yes it was. You know my father?

- *Choice #1c: Johan Lankersheim is still alive? I thought he died in the Battle of Renheiser.*
- *Choice #2c: No, but he is the reason why I left my village to travel the world. I learned many spells from his book* The Scrolls of Dark Sorcery. *It is my goal to become as skilled a sorcerer as he is.*
- *Choice #3c: Gerhardt, is that you? It's your long, lost brother Wilhelm!*

Notice that each of these responses offers vastly different story paths, almost unrelated to one another. Choice #1c implies that there is great mystery behind Johan Lankersheim. Rumors of his death have been circulating long before this encounter. Why is that the case? If you have a penchant for mystery solving, Choice #1c is the option for you. Choice #2c speaks to the player's desire for self-discovery – "I am a nascent sorcerer but I need to perfect my craft by going into the world and gaining practical knowledge even if that poses great risk to my safety." Choice #3c is about an unexpected opportunity to repair the ties with estranged family members. These are vastly different paths that may never intersect down the road. You are choosing a very different experience with each one.

These examples should give a clear picture on the basics of meaningful choice in interactive dialogue. It all boils down to the most basic of conditional statements: "If this, then that." In other words, ... "If the player chooses X, then these are the series of different responses I need to write."

Let's return to the beginning of the conversation:

> *NPC: How are you today?*

- *Choice #1a: Great. How are you?*
- *Choice #2a: Terrible. My best friend died of scurvy.*
- *Choice #3a: Shut up and get out of my way.*

<u>Player selects Choice #1a. Then –</u>

> *NPC: I'm doing well, thank you. If you are here to see Wolfgang the Shaman, please provide us the secret word.*

- *Choice #1b: Quince*
- *Choice #2b: Sassafras*
- *Choice #3b: Aha! That is a trick question. Wolfgang the Shaman requires no one to carry secrets!*

<u>Player selects Choice #1b. Then the conversation ends like so –</u>

> *NPC: I see that you are a farmer of these lands. Please sit in the section for the commoners. You will be asked to leave after 10 minutes. Thank you.*

However ...

<u>If the player selects Choice #2b, the conversation ends like so –</u>

> *NPC: Wow! I see you part of the aristocracy of this village! Please take a seat in the front row and stay as long as the Shaman wants you to stay. I bow to you in deference.*

Or ...

<u>If the player selects Choice #3b, the conversation ends like so –</u>

NPC: Nice try. Guess again.

- *Choice #1c: Quince*
- *Choice #2c: Sassafras*
- *Choice #3c: That dagger of yours? It looks familiar. Was that given to you by Johan Lankersheim?*

This branch starts off by forcing the player to restart the previous branch and choose an overtly correct answer. It's allowed in this case because the dialogue is deepening the psychology of our character. His arrogance in assuming that he was asked a trick question – and being immediately denied – indicates we're dealing with a inadvertently funny, but relatable protagonist.

The first two choices here will allow the player to enter. So let's explore Choice #3c to its end.

NPC: Why, yes it was. You know my father?

- *Choice #1d: Johan Lankersheim is still alive? I thought he died in the Battle of Renheiser.*
- *Choice #2d: No, but he is the reason why I left my village to travel the world. I learned many spells from his book* The Scrolls of Dark Sorcery. *It is my goal to become as skilled a sorcerer as he is.*
- *Choice #3d: Gerhardt, is that you? It's your long, lost brother Wilhelm!*

<u>Player selects Choice #1d. Then –</u>

NPC: He survived, but has not been the same since. If you pay him your respects, I will make sure Wolfgang the Shaman will make you a special potion. What say you?

- *Choice #1e: Next time, but today I'm in a hurry and I need the Shaman's cure for my grandmother's ill humors. The password is Quince.*
- *Choice #2e: Can't you see I'm in a hurry?!? The password is Sassafras.*
- *Choice #3e: I'd love to pay your father my respects.*

To the complete conversation tree:
If player selects Choice #1e, the NPC replies –

>   NPC: I see that you are a farmer of these lands. Please sit in the section for the commoners. You will be asked to leave after 10 minutes. Thank you.

If player selects Choice #2e, the NPC replies –

>   NPC: Well, well, well. You may be aristocracy, but outside this kingdom, you're as equal as I am. I await that day. Until then, you may take a seat in the front row and stay as long as the Shaman wants you to stay.

If player selects Choice #3e, the NPC replies –

>   NPC: Good to hear! Follow me and I will take you there.

What makes these choices strong is that you are given three different locations to experience, even if momentarily. If you selected, say, Choice #1e the first time, you have the option of exploring the other two in different gaming sessions and will experience, at the very least, two different visual environments and perspectives of Wolfgang the Shaman. Or, if you chose to see the Shaman right away, you are guaranteed two different dialogue experiences based on the class that you chose: farmer vs. aristocracy. Your gaming experience will thereby be very different in the way people treat you and what you will have access to.

Figure 2 presents a very complex breakdown of these choices in a diagram, without the notations I used above. Mapping them out visually will significantly clarify the narrative process. You will notice that when the NPC speaks (indicated in hexagons), the player character (you) will have three responses. That cadence must be continued until the end of the dialogue branch where the NPC's response or action is closely tied to your next move (e.g., exit or battle) and has exhausted further options in that conversation. It is key to keep the number of responses by the player uniform until that final moment of the branch. That's the rule-set the narrative designer establishes with the player. If you violate that rule-set out of convenience, you are cheating. It's okay if answers repeat themselves in different branches of the same conversation (that's unavoidable), but once you change the amount of player character responses, you'll have lost the faith of the player.

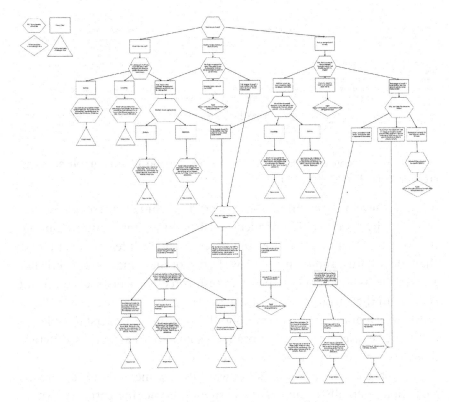

FIGURE 2 Example Branching Conversation Tree. (See full-scale version of this graph at www.crcpress.com/9781138319738.)

Why all this effort? The crux behind meaningful choice is giving a player enough content, so that he/she is compelled to replay the game through a different lens each time. Not all game narrative is in the RPG genre. But RPG elements often trickle into games that aren't, by nature, RPGs. Character customization and "choose your own adventure" decisions are part and parcel for RPGs. It's the level of depth, however, that separates a genuine RPG from a game that has light RPG elements. At minimum, RPG-light games should strive to achieve *meaningful and differentiated* content. If the choices fail to provide sufficiently distinct content or there is basically little-to-no variation among the choices in a dialogue tree, then the choices are inconsequential and cosmetic at best. The result is a weak, unambitious narrative. I'll dive into this deeper in just a moment, but first …

It is perfectly acceptable that the different choices eventually and periodically dovetail to the same story milestones. (Again, budget constraints

Act 1		
Path A (Aristocrat)	**Path B (Farmer)**	**Path C (Respectful Warrior)**
The player character sits in the front row to see Wolfgang the Shaman.	The player character sits far away to see Wolfgang the Shaman.	The player character meets Wolfgang the Shaman before his public appearance.
He offends the person sitting next to him and engages in combat.	He flirts with a woman sitting in front of him.	He offends the Shaman by insulting a reckless battle that his brother led, as it nearly caused his village to be wiped out.
He kills the stranger only to discover that the stranger was the leader of a group of violent marauders. His followers will attack the player character's village.	The father of the woman, the leader of a maurading faction, is offended and vows to scorch the player character's farm and kill everyone in his village.	The Shaman calls upon his protectors, the marauders, to wipe out the player character's village.
Dovetail moment: The player character returns to his village to stave off the attack from the mauraders.	**Dovetail moment:** The player character returns to his village to stave off the attack from the mauraders.	**Dovetail moment:** The player character returns to his village to stave off the attack from the mauraders.

FIGURE 3 Dovetail Moments. (See full-scale version of this graph at www.crcpress.com/9781138319738.)

in game development allow for modest branching.) These milestones could be the same inciting incident, crisis point, climax, and resolution. But the paths that lead to those milestones might be differentiated in tone, characters status, and points of view (POVs) of the same event. While not as extreme as different plot points, these three elements are significant changes in the narrative to encourage replayability (Figure 3).

Keeping a branching narrative slightly "on rails" is understandable. As mentioned earlier, an ambitious branching narrative has endless, differentiated content that might be too costly to execute.

Now back to the burning issue: what does a meaningful, differentiated choice actually mean? When designing branching paths, ask yourself high-level questions that focus on enhancing the player experience. For instance, if you choose Path B, what are you giving the player that is distinct from, but as entertaining as, Path A? If Path A leads to a destination that gives you a gun, but Path B leads you to the same destination that gives you a knife, you've failed at making a meaningful, differentiated choice. A different tool is cosmetic. It tells us nothing about the character's psychology nor does it reveal a new fragment of the story.

Consider a murder mystery game. Path A takes you to a crime scene through the lens of a detective. There's something odd about this detective. She's brilliant, but you can't quite trust her. Path B takes you to the same crime scene but through the lens of a young boy, who witnessed the crime. The boy notices that the detective has suspiciously taken something from the victim's pocket, yet no one saw this, but the young boy. While paths A and B might dovetail to the same locales and moments in the narrative, the different perspectives give more meaning, surprise, and breadth to the story.

If you don't have the budget to write different POVs through the lenses of two different characters, what can you do? Try limiting the experience to one character, but with different perspectives. Could the branching dialogue reveal two distinct personalities of the same detective: one that's overly forthcoming, too trusting, and emotional? Could the other be more tacit, seemingly distrustful? This isn't to say that one character is made up of two different characters. Instead, each question in the conversation tree elicits a different response from the same character, and each response reveals a different fragment of her life and psychology. "How's your mother?," for instance, could be an unhappy trigger for a character with an Electra Complex. But if that same person with an Electra Complex is asked, "How's your father?," it triggers a happy attitude. Each path, therefore, is informed by a deep, psychological driver that will influence and differentiate the choices ahead.

Different POVs from the same character (or limited set of characters) can give a cost-effective differentiation of a branching narrative. Less time is spent in crafting wholesale story beats. These different perspectives from the same character cover the same story beats, but are experienced through a different mindset and, therefore, reveal different context.

Branching narrative development can be a massive undertaking. It involves a huge time commitment as well as an extensive writing staff to pull it off. Since game companies strongly encourage replayability, branching narrative is the supplement – or even enhancement – to this customer promise. But to achieve its full potential is to lose the average player. As I describe in Chapter #11, players like the least amount of friction in their gaming experience. Story is often friction. Therefore, you cannot expect the average gamer to enjoy or even partake in branching narrative that is intricate and time-consuming. However, light branching, particularly if it triggers new and unique gameplay moments, is the ideal middle ground.

CHAPTER 8

Analysis of Narrative in Contemporary Games

WHAT ARE THE CRITERIA OF WELL-TOLD NARRATIVE IN GAMES?

Up to this point, I've provided copious details on crafting solid story structure and creating compelling worlds and characters. These will be useful when we examine the stories of two video games in this chapter. But before we do, it's important to establish additional criteria for what qualifies as a solid game narrative. These can vary from studio to studio, but I always keep in mind the following:

- Are the story milestones exciting and/or compelling?

- Is the character development organic and gradual?

- Does the narrative have a relationship to the gameplay or is it independent of it? To what degree if the latter? Do the actions from the narrative have consequences on the gameplay? Does the gameplay have consequences on the narrative?

- Is the narrative frictionless? Or is the fun being interrupted too many times in order for me to follow a story that is not interesting?

- Does the story fit with the rest of the game? Is it tonally consistent? Is the pacing consistent?

- Most importantly …

AM I EMOTIONALLY INVESTED?

One of the major issues with games is a player's lack of emotional attachment to the story and characters. Oftentimes, a non-playable character (NPC) can serve a functional purpose, thus justifying his/her need in your gaming experience. This type of NPC could be someone who provides you with information about the locale or mission upon which you are about to embark. Other functions include: healing (someone who gives you medicine to recover from an injury); equipping (someone who gives you weapons); momentary saving (someone who gives you shelter from combat); assisting (someone who joins you in combat and provides cover). The list goes on. But as you can see, these roles render the character as a device of usage. A player will typically ask themselves, *How can I use them in a way to expedite my journey?*

This isn't to say the gaming experience makes a player manipulative or indifferent to human emotion. It is instead an experience that, by design, forces the player to use everything at their disposal to move forward without stopping.

Accordingly, within those functions, seldom is there an opportunity to get to know those NPCs. Or, if they are along with you for your entire journey, it is rare that you'll get a chance to know them in a way that, upon their absence or death, will evoke feelings of loss or sadness.

There are exceptions of course. In *Fable II*, a dog is your faithful companion throughout the game. However, after it dies taking a bullet for you (before being resurrected later on), the world coarsens. The protagonist is no longer a child, but a hero on a mission. Likewise, in *The Last of Us* (which I will delve into later), the death of the protagonist's young daughter in the beginning changes our hero permanently. It sets him on a path that is emotionally indifferent at first, but then reverses once the stakes of survival involve the saving of another girl.

Emotional investment is tricky. What is defined as emotional investment may be different from player to player. The loss of a functional character might spur a player's despair. Now they have no one to rely on for that function, and therefore their series of missions will be harder to accomplish.

But this is the important distinction: loss should not evoke a player's annoyance due to the absence of a function. A true emotional connection is not about making your job easier; it is about making your experience more meaningful and fulfilling. A character's presence ought to provide joy; their absence, sorrow.

If genuine emotion doesn't arise, then the character was either not written well enough or, by design, he/she was strictly a functional device.

A writer's or narrative designer's goals are to transcend an NPC from function to meaningful investment.

WHY DO GAMES FAIL AT TELLING EMOTIONAL STORIES?

This is a difficult question not because it's hard to identify, but because it puts into light the consumer and developer.

Games are an addictive activity. The products are designed to keep players' buttoning on the controller for hours on end. The dopamine release upon every buttoning activity (e.g., killing an enemy, avoiding gunfire, making a goal, or jumping from building to building) satisfies a primordial impulse in all of us. Accordingly, to tap into these primordial impulses relentlessly is to experience endless joy … at least in terms of addiction.

But these twitch-muscle activities do not allow a player to absorb and reflect upon the environment for anything more than the length of time that the immediate mission allows you. There is no epicurean stop-and-smell-the-roses moment. Games create grinding experiences. An art museum or a theater experience (i.e., traditional art) is the complete opposite. In the latter category, a viewer experiences a slower, more methodical process to absorb the stimuli around him/her.

Games are fast; traditional art is slow. Games are about instant gratification; traditional art is about long-term enrichment. Games are about following directions; traditional art is about making arbitrary interpretations. Games have a definitive set of rules and a victory state; traditional art is unspecific until it's part of the public discourse where its meaning is debated *ad nauseam*.

People play games, generally, not for an emotional experience. They play to have fun. And oftentimes, fun is not about cerebral issues, but about light, fast, and accessible subject matter. That's why the hero's journey remains a tried-and-true model for game narrative.

However, this isn't to say we should give games a pass when it comes to emotional investment. There are opportunities to do so (as mentioned in the examples given earlier), where emotion can still fit within the gaming experience.

This isn't just about the consumer. They might expect a light, non-cerebral experience because that's what they've been fed for so many years! Game creators expect or even aim for light experiences too. They grew up on games. In fact, games might have been their primary (and sometimes only) diet of media. Therefore, it's no surprise that the medium's lack of emotional investment corresponds to the developers' lack of exposure to media with emotional investment.

Additionally, many of these folks have a narrow pool of interests when it comes to story. *Star Wars*, *Game of Thrones*, *Harry Potter*, and *The Lord of the Rings* are (obviously) great franchises, but they are the most prevalent go-to examples in most narrative brainstorming sessions. (Well, those and superhero movies.) To limit oneself to a narrow pool of stories and genres is to increase the likelihood that one's game narrative will be stale and cliché.

But emotion is not the main reason why these franchises are beloved. Rich characters, worlds, and action scenes continue to evoke loyalty and zeal from fans and developers alike. They can also overshadow the sentiment shared between characters. Thus, if there is no awareness of emotional moments in these intellectual properties (IPs), then there is no chance that emotional moments will cross one's mind when developing the narrative.

That's why it's crucial to involve writers and narrative designers in the brainstorming phase of creating an IP. Their openness to emotional moments and their experience in writing for other fiction-driven media make them invaluable. If they cannot lead the discussions in IP creation, then they need to be the "story whisperer" to every creative director or lead designer who does.

GAME NARRATIVE BREAKDOWN EXAMPLES

I've chosen two games to illustrate how the elements of narrative come together in an actual product in the marketplace. Story milestones, components of great character and world building, and emotional investment touchstones are the driving criteria. The following two games are vastly different in genre as well as in the quality of storytelling. One is a masterpiece in game narrative; the other, a Hollywood-bloated misfire.

NBA 2K16

Studio: Visual Concepts

Publisher: 2K Sports (a subsidiary of Take-Two Interactive)

Writers: Spike Lee, Alrick Brown, Barry Michael Cooper, Rhys Jones, Julius Pryor IV, Kiel Adrian Scott, Sean Michael Sullivan, Tor Unsworth

Year Published: 2015

Premise

A young basketball phenom nicknamed "The Freq" is on the verge of becoming the next superstar of the National Basketball Association

(NBA). But a friend from his past damages his reputation off the court, causing dissension within his family and the team owner.

In a Nutshell

Upon its release, *NBA 2K16* was the latest installment in one of the industry's best-selling franchises in the last decade, *NBA 2K*. This time, Take-Two Interactive upped the ante by offering a story mode (called "Livin' Da Dream") written and directed by Spike Lee.

The legendary filmmaker admitted in the game's "extras" feature that video games were a new experience for him. Did it pay off?

Main Characters

Frequency Vibrations aka The Freq – a basketball phenom since high school, Freq continues to excel in college and makes his way to the NBA as the hottest rookie in his draft class. Achieving all the accolades and fame that come with being a superstar, the Freq navigates the pressures of the league with the help of his fraternal twin sister, his girlfriend, and his agent. He is deeply trusting of those around him and expects the same in return. In addition to his near superhuman athleticism, he is a man of honor and loyalty and exercises kindness to those in his close circle, particularly to his parents who gave him everything with the little they had. Due to his extraordinary skill on the court and ability to command instant adoration from those around him, Freq is the narrative's protagonist.

Vic Van Lier – Freq's best friend since childhood. Vic is always finding himself in trouble and relies on Freq to bail him out. However, by the time Freq makes it to the NBA, Vic's hijinks escalate, including spending an exorbitant amount of Freq's money; talking trash about players on social media; and getting caught drunk on video after being stopped by the police. Eventually, his shenanigans force Freq to choose between his friend and his team.

Yvette Ming Ching – Freq's girlfriend. Ever since they dated, she's capitalized on Freq's fame to catapult her own career in the fashion industry. But unlike Vic, Yvette wants nothing but the best for Freq and has proven to be an invaluable advocate for his career. She is often at odds with Freq's sister, Cee-Cee, who doesn't trust Yvette because she believes Yvette is just after his fame and money. However, it's likely the case that she's jealous of Yvette because of her closeness to him.

Cee-Cee – Freq's fraternal twin sister. As soon as the NBA is interested in drafting the Freq, Cee-Cee steps in as his business manager. The role, at first, is too much for her to handle as she struggles to make the right business decisions for Freq, but she eventually comes into her own. She's at the center of a lot of rifts inside Freq's inner circle, including with his girlfriend and his agent. All she wants to do is protect her brother.

Dom Pagnotti – super agent in the sports world. He is Freq's fast-talking, savvy deal-maker. While he comes across as slick and untrustworthy, he turns out to be Freq's compass through the murky waters of sports business. He always has Freq's best interests in mind even if it defies Cee-Cee's expectations. He will do whatever it takes to build his client's reputation and get him the best deal possible.

Pete and Martha – Freq's kind, selfless parents. Freq is devoutly loyal to his parents, even involving them in press conferences. There isn't a specific archetype they represent; they are, rather, a device. They humanize the superhero, make him relatable in ways that Freq could not do himself.

Team Owner – wealthy, intense, no-bullshit owner, who pushes Freq to conform to the standards of his team. On the court is one thing; off the court is another. His players must represent the team gallantly, on and off the court. This poses a problem when Vic constantly hangs out with the team, exploits Freq's popularity, and embarrasses himself in public. The owner forces Freq to take sides eventually: it's either the team or Vic.

Key Story Beats
Act 1

Introduction to Protagonist's Purpose – when playing basketball on a local neighborhood court, Freq, a high school student, reveals his goal to make it to the NBA. When Vic pops up, Freq reveals that his loyalty to his family and friends is a personal priority. In this scene, Freq reveals a professional and personal purpose. Vic's mischievousness is clear and serves to foreshadow events to come.

Inciting Incident – Freq's dominant performance at a high school game puts him on the radar of college scouts. However, this one game implies that Freq's excellence was an aggregation over years of playing at a high level.

Refuse the Call – not applicable here. However, one could interpret Freq's listening to numerous college recruiters' pitches and not accepting them as a refusal of a call. He's waiting for all offers to net out before making a decision. This reveals a positive character trait of Freq's: that he's patient and thoughtful. In this game, this narrative beat is more like "Not committing to the call."

Situation Worsens – during Freq's last game in high school, Vic is riding off the coattails of his superstar buddy as an FOF – Friend of Freq – by making deals with shady people. Once again, this is a stronger foreshadowing beat than anything else. Freq's decision to commit to a college is agnostic to whatever shady deals Vic is making; nonetheless, that shadiness will put our hero in a difficult situation come the next act.

Accept the Call – Freq makes an announcement in a home video in front of his family and Vic about the college he will commit to. (The cut scene adjusts to the choice the player makes.) This beat reinforces Freq's "Introduction to Protagonist's Purpose" by making a huge decision that leads him closer to getting to the NBA (professional purpose) and by showing his love and devotion to his family in making that decision (personal purpose).

Point of No Return – a one-on-one conversation with Freq's mom (*ala* docu-style confessional room with the director) reveals how this new step fulfills the dreams and expectations she has had of him since he was young. Now Freq is on his way. This makes Freq's journey not only about him, but also about his family. Should he succeed, we will feel the joy that the family feels. Should he miss the boat, we will feel the same grave disappointment that they will feel.

Act 2

Adjustment to New World – Freq's college experience is compressed narratively. It's strictly a device, in that it is just a realistic waystation to the NBA, but offers no character development or interesting story beats to enhance dramatic conflict.

But after winning the championship in college, Freq makes a decision with his agent Pagnotti about Freq's draft strategy, including his leaving school early. The decision is discussed over speaker phone with his parents, sister, and new girlfriend, Yvette. Pagnotti's suggestion to leave college early goes against what the family wanted Freq to do. But this is a unique opportunity based on his unique talent. The traditional path will not get him to where he wants to be. This is the new cutthroat world of the business of sports, no longer the neighborhood playground. The decision to stay or leave college is debated among Freq's close circle. While there's no unanimous answer, Freq decides to leave college early, sign with Pagnotti, and get ready for the draft. Vic's presence in his life is also a cause for debate, as it might affect his draft position.

Vic eventually gets drafted (the draft position depends on player performance in previous games). He signs with his new team in front of an enthusiastic press conference.

Escalating Burdens – now that Freq is an official NBA player, everything starts to change for him, including Vic's recklessness and its effect it will have on his team. The team owner takes this to heart and tells Freq to watch out.

Exposure of Weakness – in the same scene, the owner reveals a filmed arrest of a drunken Vic. He's an embarrassment to Freq and to the team. Freq paid $100,000 to lawyers to make the incident go away. The owner says Vic is banned from the facilities and will arrest him if he's seen anywhere near the team. If Freq helps Vic defy those orders, the owner will cut him from the team. Freq has no choice but to comply because, as he discovers, a morality clause in his contract will hurt him detrimentally.

Loss of Trust – video game players, at this point, should have a sense of doubt about Freq's judgment. If he can't keep his friend in line and instead spends exorbitant amounts of money to free him from an arrest, what kind of leader or hero is the Freq?

Midpoint/Low Point – Freq's inner circle focuses on how to make him a brand outside of the court. But how to do it forces dissension among the ranks. Cee-Cee's distrust of Yvette and Pagnotti culminates. Pushed too far, Freq lashes out at everyone and doles out orders to Dom, Cee-Cee, and Yvette on how to proceed. He steps up and assumes the role of what's expected of him: a leader.

In the Belly of Jonah's whale – Vic tries to create distrust with Cee-Cee and Dom and says the streets do not approve of how Freq's taking his career. His Jordan sneakers are not being bought, which is a colossal failure. Vic implies that he's a better business confidant than those within Freq's inner circle. When Cee-Cee intercedes, Yvette pushes back and schools her on her terrible promotional strategy for the Jordan shoes. Chaos ensues. Cee-Cee offers a new strategy and proposes to be his "manager." Freq is not cool with that, as he thinks this is a money grab for his sister. Freq's inner circle implodes.

Redemption Path Begins – in the same scene, Cee-Cee reveals she does not appreciate when Yvette and Vic are prioritized over her. Freq convinces her that he doesn't need to be protected anymore by her. She needs to accept them. Cee-Cee acquiesces, but only once he reveals that he knows Yvette and Vic are using him. Freq asserts that he's using them just as much.

Act 3

Ticking Time Bomb Introduced – Vic confronts Freq about why he won't financially support his new endeavor as a hip-hop artist. When Freq denies him, Vic loses his cool by expressing his jealousy over Freq's better upbringing. When Vic doesn't let up, Freq unloads on him, saying he's had enough of his behavior. Vic's leeching is out of control. To top it off, he made a pass at Yvette! The Freq has spent over $250,000 on legal fees and frivolous parties for Vic – and for what? Once Vic feels unappreciated, he blackmails his friend in revealing an old secret: the mysterious death of Dirtbike Donnie. An accidental fall down a stairwell led to his death, and Freq was the cause. Vic covered it up and claims Freq is indebted to him forever. Freq doesn't deny it. Vic then guilts Freq into letting him borrow his expensive car so that he can screw around and have fun. With his emotional stranglehold over the Freq, Vic now has carte blanche to do whatever he wants.

Escalating Burdens Intensify – after a practice is let out early, Freq struggles with his friend's behavior through a time-lapsed montage. Meanwhile, his relationship with Yvette gets stronger.

Obligatory Scene/Climax – the team's owner has a sit-down with the Freq and his inner circle to revisit the off-court shenanigans of Vic. His behavior has gotten worse after a social media insult toward a teammate went viral. Freq, Cee-Cee, and Pagnotti get defensive after the owner makes a veiled threat to cut Freq from the team. Freq stands up for Vic – but Cee-Cee, Dom, and the owner are unified: dump Vic. Freq makes the decision to leave the team.

Reversal – after becoming a free agent, Freq talks with Pagnotti about his next move. Off-screen, Freq promised Pagnotti that he would cut off ties with Vic. He reveals in this scene that he couldn't, due to loyalty. The Freq vows not to make his next move without talking to Vic first.

Recognition – in a press conference, Freq will announce the next team he will play for. But first he shares that the decision was made with the help of Yvette, Cee-Cee, and his parents. He reinforces that their love and trust made this decision possible. This is now the first time where the professional and personal goals intersect. Beforehand, it was expressed as two separate goals in the same scene; here, his professional goal could not have been possible without his personal goal. Vic, being suspiciously off the radar for days, was not part of this process.

Resolution of Bomb – post-press conference, Freq gets a call from a police officer. Vic died as a result of speeding in Freq's car, which spun out of control and crashed.

Denouement – after Vic's funeral in their hometown, Freq and Cee-Cee reflect on how "life's a trip" – nothing could prepare them for the curveballs of life. They then meet up with their folks, where Freq shares his appreciation for them, particularly their involvement in his life. After Freq and Cee-Cee leave, they surprise their parents with a gift: keys to a new house and tickets to Montego Bay.

As a post-script, Vic reads from a letter he wrote to Freq, presumably right before he died. He shares how painful his childhood was, particularly regarding his mother who died of AIDS. He thanks Freq for finding love through his family. All he wanted was to be loved and feel a sense of belonging.

Please note: While the letter is recited and performed by Vic, it's not understood if it's read by Freq or if it's just an inelegantly placed narrative device to give Vic one last say. Why Vic wrote this note remains unclear. This moment is, in Aristotelian dramatic terms, a catharsis. However, it is recited by a supporting character and not by the protagonist. Its presence, therefore, doesn't make much sense except to force players to feel a certain way.

Positives of the Narrative

The dialogue was natural and authentic and allowed for the actors to give seamless performances.

Negatives of the Narrative

This game's only narrative mechanisms were cut scenes. As I've written about earlier, cut scenes are not beloved by the majority of gamers. Remember: they do not like friction in their gaming experience. What's worse, these cut scenes were 8–10 minutes long! No gamer, even a lover of narrative, will have patience for that. It feels like the publisher was so excited to have a premiere filmmaker as part of their next game that they gave him free rein to do whatever he wanted and turned a blind eye to the needs of gamers.

The type of story that was told is your run-of-the-mill "rags to riches" trope, which is common in the sports genre. It tires very quickly. But that's not the key problem with the narrative here.

First, there is an extremely loose/almost non-existent relationship to gameplay. With the exception of selecting your college team or forcing a trade to another NBA team, the actions you make in the narrative have no bearing on what happens on the court. Similarly, what happens on the court is not even recognized in the cut scenes. It would have been nice to lose a crucial game and see what the reaction is in the cut scene. But there was none of that. In fact, it didn't matter what you did on the court; the cut scenes were going to continue with a story that was less about you as a basketball player and more about how business decisions can affect personal relationships. Not a bad foundation for a sports drama, but not compelling enough for a video game. It meshes well with neither the fast-paced nature of the sport nor the gameplay expectations from fans.

There was another major, glaring issue. Players can customize their character in the very beginning of the game. You can choose your height, your weight, and your hair style. You can even choose your race. Freq's parents and twin sister are African American. But a player could easily make their character Asian, White, or Latino as well as African American. If the player customizes their character to be a different race or ethnicity than the Freq's family, this game will not adjust to that choice. So, if you customized the Freq to be, for instance, Asian American, he will still have two parents and a fraternal twin sister who are African American. Consequences have actions, and player choice is completely ignored in this narrative.

Second, the dramatic structure falls apart halfway through the story after Vic emotionally blackmails Freq with an incident from their past. If Freq listens to the owner and cuts ties with Vic entirely, Vic will (or so he threatens) expose that Freq killed a local thief called Dirtbike Donnie after a struggle on a stairwell. Freq claimed it was an accident, but Vic never believed him. In fact, he will hold that secret over Freq's head to exploit all the access and riches that come with being a superstar hanger-on.

This is a huge shift in our perception of Vic, who, at first, came across as a lovable yet troubled friend that couldn't get out of his own way. It calls into question Freq's dogged loyalty to keeping Vic around, despite the owner's disagreement. Was all of his loyalty and goodwill toward Vic a charade? Was the Freq living in fear of blackmail this entire time?

Not likely. After Vic dies in a car accident, Freq honors him at his funeral and is genuinely distraught over his friend's death.

Also, the blackmail card was never used or mentioned after that story beat, which would normally be classified as the low point. Freq continued on with his career without fear or even acknowledgment that Vic had something over him. *In other words, there were no consequences to that story beat.* Why was it even there? Why were we forced to question our hero's integrity and intelligence?

When Vic dies, it's more of a relief than a tragedy. He made our hero look bad on so many occasions, even before he tried to blackmail him. Vic is not a character for whom we should have sympathy. This is a failure in storytelling, mainly because Spike Lee set up the rules for the characters early on and then broke them halfway through. Are we to trust what these characters have to say or do after that? Not likely.

Third, there isn't a real antagonist in this story. Yes, Freq has to make tough, even unfair decisions at the command of his team's owner, but those choices didn't thwart Freq's career or spoil his relationships. Vic might be the closest to an antagonist, simply because he spoils the Freq's reputation and forces him to take sides against his owner. But Vic never really affected his career on the court, nor did he push him away from his family or girlfriend. Vic was basically a nuisance, but not a significant enough opposing force to genuinely obstruct our hero's path.

In Conclusion

NBA 2K16 has a well-intentioned narrative with high production values. But behind its good intentions are deeply flawed structural missteps and characters that are ultimately uneven. Yet, it's important to discuss this game because the video game industry tends to have a secret love affair with Hollywood. So often do publishers and studios go after marquee talent as a misguided strategy to increase sales of the game. But a movie star or popular filmmaker whose name is on the cover is never an enhancement to sales. Gamers don't care about movie stars; they care about great gameplay.

And it is often the case that the exorbitant money a publisher spends on a famous actor or filmmaker takes away from other elements of game development. Such is also the case when well-respected screenwriters of film and television are hired to write the story of a video game. Many of these writers have zero experience in game narrative or in playing games. Much of their work will be thrown away, and game writers and narrative designers will have to come in and change over 90% of the writing. That's why, today, many of these Hollywood writers, by fiat of the game studio, will collaborate early and steadily with narrative designers to make their work more "game friendly."

Luckily, these types of engagements don't happen that often because the return on investment is very low. Nonetheless, the temptation to hire Hollywood talent exists and should be met with great caution.

THE LAST OF US (2013)

Studio: Naughty Dog

Publisher: Sony Interactive Entertainment

Writer: Neil Druckmann

Year Published: 2013

Premise

An outbreak from a poisonous fungus spreads across the United States. People morph into zombie-like creatures known as "The Infected." Twenty years later, America has become a post-apocalyptic wasteland, where a paramilitary force rules with an iron fist. Cult-like factions rebel against their oppressive rules within quarantine zones where survivors are forced to live. Joel, a cynic who lost his daughter in the first moments of the outbreak, makes ends meet by being a smuggler of goods from one zone to the next. When he's presented with a new challenge of taking a young girl to a quarantine zone across the country where she holds the cure to this zombie-like disease, Joel must face his darkest demons and assume the role of father figure once again.

In a Nutshell

The Last of Us was a huge hit of 2013. The game sold over 7 million units in its first 13 months. By 2018, the game sold over 17 million units for both PS3 and PS4.*

It was also critically acclaimed, recognized especially for its writing. Naughty Dog, a Sony studio based in Santa Monica, CA, was known for their highly successful *Uncharted* franchise. With this new IP led by game director and head writer Neil Druckmann, the studio proved that it wasn't a one-trick pony. They also proved that they are the best studio in the world for game narrative.

Main Characters

Joel – a rugged cynic who knows all the angles on how to survive in post-apocalyptic America. Joel lost his daughter during the first hours of the outbreak. Twenty years later, he is a smuggler-for-hire who seldom gets emotionally attached to any person or any cause. That is, until Ellie walks into his life.

---

* (Sarkar 2018)

Ellie – the new daughter figure for Joel. She holds the key to the cure of the outbreak that has infected millions. Tissue from her brain can be used to create a vaccine. She will need to be delivered safely to a lab to conduct this experiment. It is likely she will not survive this procedure.

Marlene – head of the unscrupulous Fireflies, a rebel group who believes they have the cure to the outbreak.

Bill – curmudgeon; booby trap creator; mechanic; prepper and survivalist.

David – leader of a group of random survivors that compete for resources with Joel and Ellie. Many of his men were killed months earlier by Joel. When he discovers Ellie hunting nearby, he subtly plans to exact revenge.

Key Story Beats

Act 1

Introduction to Protagonist's Purpose – Joel reveals to his young daughter Sarah that he's about to lose a contracting job. They connect after she gives him a watch for his birthday. We know from the very beginning that Joel's emotional purpose is being a good dad.

Inciting Incident – later that evening, a mysterious pandemic hits their region of the United States (the South). Of what nature, we do not know at first; however, Joel attempts to drive out of town with Sarah but is seized by zombie-like townspeople before getting into a car accident. When he comes to, he carries Sarah to the streets while chaos ensues. A military officer confronts them, thinking they are one of the zombie-like townspeople, and shoots at both of them. Sarah is killed nearly instantly.

The story flashes forward to twenty years later. The world is a post-apocalyptic wasteland under martial law.

Refuse the Call – after infiltrating a seedy underground of a local kingpin named Robert, Joel joins his friend Tess in trying to retrieve guns that Robert gave away to the mysterious faction known as the Fireflies. After Tess and Joel rough him up, Robert tells them to kill the Fireflies and get their guns back. When talking to a Firefly who claims to have access to the guns, Joel doesn't believe that she has them, so she tells Joel and Tess to follow her to an abandoned building where they'll get the guns. In exchange, they must smuggle contraband out of the quarantine zone to a new one across the country. They discover that the contraband is a 14-year-old girl named Ellie. Joel agrees to take her to the tunnel to wait for Tess and Marlene, but refuses to escort Ellie to this new quarantine zone. Although

Ellie might be the key to finding a vaccine to the virus, Joel can't trust Marlene, mainly because she's a Firefly.

Situation Worsens – smuggling Ellie out of the military zone is dangerous as soldiers attempt to stop them. But Tess kills two soldiers after Ellie stabs one of them. They discover, through one of the dead soldier's instruments, that Ellie is infected. Tess and Joel think Marlene set them up. When more soldiers arrive, Joel, Tess, and Ellie have to escape the sector at all costs or they will die.

Ellie reveals that while there are quarantine zones with their own potential cures to the virus, she is the sole link to finding a vaccine.

When trying to escape, they get attacked by infected townspeople (now known as Clickers) and must undertake various physical challenges.

Accept the Call – when the person at the drop-off location is dead, Joel finds out that Tess, his beloved friend and partner, is infected. Joel succumbs to taking the girl to the far-off quarantine zone, so that he can help find the cure for the remaining uninfected people in the country.

Point of No Return – Tess stays behind so that Joel and Ellie can escape. Tess dies in the process. Escaping to the other side of this quarantine zone requires one last perilous journey of killing hostile soldiers and more physical challenges (that become harder with Ellie's inability to swim). With the future of humanity resting on his shoulders, Joel knows what his professional goal is: bring Ellie to the lab in the far-off quarantine zone so that a vaccine can be created. His renewed personal goal emerges as well: Ellie is gradually fulfilling a daughter role, triggering Joel's instincts as a father.

Act 2

Adjustment to New World – Joel sets the ground rules with Ellie about their relationship: Don't mention Tess and don't tell anyone about her own condition, for fear that she will be killed. They travel through the outside world, where Ellie has never seen the woods before due to the fact that she's been sequestered inside Sector 12 (the quarantine zone they just fled) for her entire life.

Escalating Burdens – Joel and Ellie look for his friend Bill, who can get them a car that they can use to travel across the country. In this search, they come across various physical challenges, booby traps, and armed confrontations but learn to get closer to one another and work with each other.

After meeting with Bill, Joel realizes that they need to gather various parts from cars that can be used to build a working car. Bill joins Ellie and Joel on this quest. This involves more confrontations (including a new creature called Bloaters) and physical challenges.

When Ellie and Joel get the newly refurbished car working, Joel and Ellie develop a stronger father/daughter bond. But when they are ambushed by a gang of non-infected people (also known as Hunters) on an alternate highway, they're forced to abandon their car and hit the road by foot, where they must make it to a bridge in the distance. More physical challenges (including an awesome elevator shaft scene) and confrontations take place. Joel eludes the Hunters, but in doing so, the in-game dialogue foreshadows more confrontations to come. Ellie saves Joel by shooting a Hunter who attempted to drown Joel under an overflow of water in an abandoned building. Joel resents being saved by her (or by anyone for that matter). The bitter exchange between the two resembles a heated yet frivolous exchange between a parent and child. However, this time the person with "attitude" is the parent.

Their bond increases when Joel teaches Ellie how to fire a shotgun as they travel through enemy territory of the hunters.

Along the way, Joel and Ellie meet two strangers – Henry and his younger brother Sam – who are doing their best to survive each day. They agree to join Henry and Sam on their way to a hideout, which overlooks the aforementioned bridge. This scene offers more opportunities for Joel and Ellie to increase their bond, fight off enemies, and undertake physical challenges.

The four of them decide to get to the bridge late at night. When a ladder accidentally falls to the ground leaving Joel stranded underneath the bridge, Henry and Sam can't do anything to help Joel. They encourage Ellie to join them and abandon Joel out of self-preservation. But Ellie refuses and drops down beneath the bridge to be with Joel, as Henry and Sam rush off. Ellie and Joel must survive a harrowing showdown with the military who is guarding the bridge. They drop below to the water and are swept to the other side of the bridge, but not before Joel gets knocked out.

When he comes to at the other end, Joel is face-to-face with Henry. Joel puts his gun on Henry as a response to abandoning him at the bridge. They quickly work out their issues in an effort to track down a communications tower.

They encounter more attacks from Clickers and more physical challenges. A drop-down gate forces a separation between the characters: Henry and Ellie as one group; Joel and Sam as the other. Each side must work together and find their way back to each other in a dark abandoned building with Clickers everywhere. This reinforces Joel's instinct of being a parent: he reflexively protects Sam with every threat that pops up. When all four reunite, they set their eyes on getting closer to the communications tower. But first, Joel steps up as a protector of everyone around him to shield them from a series of harrowing encounters with the Clickers.

Joel then offers Henry a chance to find and join up with the Fireflies. If they can make it to Wyoming, Joel's brother (a Firefly) can do the rest.

After a harrowing encounter with more Clickers, Joel serves as a sharpshooter for the others to help them get to another safe haven. Finally, it's a moment to breathe as Joel lets his guard down and connects with Henry. At the same time, Ellie bonds with Sam and reveals her fears of ending up alone. This is one of the only moments in the game where the pace is slowed down to bolster the emotional connection between these characters. Therefore, if tragedy were to strike anyone of them, the player will feel something significant. Case in point ...

Sam turns into an infected being and attacks Ellie. To save her life, Henry kills his younger brother. Henry then turns the gun on himself and commits suicide.

Later ... Joel reunites with his brother Tommy at a deactivated power plant and meets his new wife Maria. Tommy and others have made the power plant a micro-civilization made up of 20 families. In a one-on-one with Tommy, Joel wants his brother to take Ellie off his hands and deliver her to the Fireflies and collect the payment. In exchange, Joel wants some gear. The two argue but put their differences on hold when they are attacked by bandits looking to steal resources. Afterwards, Tommy agrees to take Ellie to the Fireflies. Joel starts to head back home.

Exposure of Weakness – Joel, realizing that the mission to take Ellie to the lab is too dangerous, turns around and heads back to Tommy's. It's not out of a sense of duty, but rather a subconscious desire to be a parent and relive his life with his daughter. He suppresses practicality and self-preservation to be a dad. And this could kill him.

Loss of Trust – after discovering that Joel almost abandoned her, Ellie steals Tommy's horse and escapes to a ranch. When Joel finds her, she confronts Joel. *What are you afraid of,* she asks him? She then brings up the memory of his daughter and forces him to admit that he wants to give up on her because he's afraid to lose another person in his life. Joel tells her they must go their separate ways.

Midpoint/Low Point – minutes later, the ranch gets raided by bandits. Joel, Tommy, and Ellie trek back by horse to the power plant. Joel has second thoughts and decides to continue on the path he set forth and will deliver Ellie to the Fireflies lab at the University of Eastern Colorado (where the experiment on Ellie to find a cure will be conducted). But when they arrive at the lab, no one is there. However, someone left a voice recording that reveals that the Fireflies have moved to Utah.

Joel gets impaled during a fight with random thugs at the university. Ellie must save him by pulling metal debris off of him. Joel steadily loses consciousness while escaping the university. He relies on Ellie to help him through, but then he blacks out.

In the Belly of Jonah's whale – many months have passed and Ellie finds herself in the darkest days of winter. She has become a formidable warrior in the wild. The player's point of view (POV) has shifted from Joel to Ellie. She confronts two men. The leader, known as David, will exchange antibiotics for a deer she just killed. After one of his men goes off to retrieve the antibiotics, Ellie and David must defend themselves against an attack by an infected horde. When they do so successfully, David reveals that his group of friends were killed by a man who fits Joel's physical description. Ellie recoils when the other man returns and holds a gun to her head. But it's a fake threat. David tells her that she and Joel won't survive much longer in this winter. The two men take off, leaving Ellie frightened of the grim reality that awaits.

Joel has gotten progressively worse since the impaling incident at the University of Eastern Colorado. Ellie is doing everything in her power to care for his needs.

The men who approached Ellie for food in exchange for antibiotics seize her safe haven with Joel and attempt to kill her. As she defends herself, she shows how much she has evolved into a survivor and stone-cold killer. Eventually, David overtakes her and abducts her.

When a severely weak Joel discovers that she's gone, he goes out to find her in the brutal winter. (The player's POV shifts again, returning to Joel.) In his search, the men that seized their safe haven attempt to mow him down. Joel takes one of the men captive and tortures him to reveal the whereabouts of Ellie.

Meanwhile, Ellie attempts to escape from David's base in the middle of a snowstorm with no weapons or other resources. (Player POV shifts back to Ellie during this escape.) But David corners her in an abandoned steakhouse; she attempts to elude him as he shoots at her. The steakhouse catches on fire, narrowing Ellie's chances of survival.

Joel trudges along in the bitter cold and eventually finds David's base. He kills many of his men along the way, even as the winter conditions intensify. Joel refuses to give up; finding Ellie is critical.

Joel reunites with Ellie right as she is stabbing David to death.

Act 3

Redemption Path Begins – months later, it's springtime, and Joel and Ellie are getting closer to the lab. But there's something off about Ellie. She seems distracted, less motivated to soldier on, less in sync with Joel. There's a glimmer of hope when they come across a giraffe eating foliage and grass in an abandoned lot.

Ticking Time Bomb Introduced – Joel stops to let Ellie know that they don't have to go forward with this; they can go back to Tommy's. Ellie moves forward; after all they've been through, it can't be for nothing.

Escalating Burdens Intensify – they press on. Ellie shows him a picture of his daughter. This hits Joel hard. He says he can't escape his past.

They undertake various physical acts and encounter more hostility from the infected.

An underwater incident involving a submerged bus forces Joel and Ellie to swim through a maze before they get to air. When they do, they are surrounded by the Fireflies. Joel is attacked and knocked unconscious.

Obligatory Scene/Climax – when he regains consciousness, Ellie is nowhere to be seen. He comes face-to-face with Marlene, head of the Fireflies, who questions Joel on how he got this far. Joel attributes that to Ellie's resolve. Marlene reveals that Ellie is being prepped for surgery. The process to create the cure has begun. Marlene also reveals that the reason why Ellie is the basis for the cure is because of a growth inside her head. This will serve as the foundation for the vaccine. However, removing the growth will likely kill her.

Joel rejects this and says he'll just take Ellie back home. But it's too late; this is what's best for society and there's nothing he can do about it. Joel is beaten down by a Firefly soldier.

Joel eventually disarms the soldier, shoots him, and finds out the whereabouts of the operating room right before the soldier dies. Joel heads toward the operating room and kills all those who get in his way.

Reversal – when he gets to the operating room, he shoots the surgeon and rescues Ellie. But her condition is untenable. It's unclear if she's dying or drugged.

After escaping to an empty parking lot, Joel carries an unconscious Ellie in his arms. Marlene stops him by aiming a gun right at him. Just as she's about to shoot …

Resolution of Bomb – we cut to Joel, who is driving Ellie away from the hospital. A flashback reveals what happened during his confrontation with Marlene. Joel shot her, as he cannot risk any of the Fireflies coming after Ellie, even if that means the lives of millions hang in the balance.

In the car ride, he lies to Ellie and says the Fireflies stopped looking for a cure. When they return to Tommy's place, Ellie is not herself. She's slower. Her skin is showing signs of infection.

Recognition – Ellie confronts Joel about what the Fireflies told him. *Is that true?* Joel lies and tells her "Yes."

Denouement – the game ends on a fabricated moment of uncertainty. Ellie thinks there is no hope, no chance for a cure. Joel cannot tell her the truth and risk losing her, even if that means saving the lives of others. But it reinforces the message that Joel, who had given up on being a parent after the death of his daughter, has been reawakened as a dad. The connection to Sarah (through Ellie) has come full circle. Even though Ellie and Joel are not blood related, their bond is just as strong as any biological father and daughter could ever have. And this connection, as Joel realizes, is sacrosanct. Nothing will come between them, even if it's for the greater good.

Positives of the Narrative

The story is simple: deliver girl to safety. It's the difficulty in achieving this goal, however, which makes the game both an exciting adventure as well as an emotionally wrought father–daughter drama. Survival is the common thread in this game. As such, the slightest threat to either Joel or Ellie is emotionally jarring. If Joel dies, his new daughter figure will not reach safety. If she dies, Joel will relive the trauma of the loss of his biological daughter from twenty years earlier. The consequences here are not just about the logistics of safety; they are about the sanctity of family at its most rudimentary level. This kind of emotional depth is seldom seen in any medium today. For games, it's a triumph.

Additionally, the in-game dialogue is crafted masterfully. When you explore the post-apocalyptic world, you see its various conditions and the harsh treatment that the military pays its citizens. While your focus is not necessarily on what minor characters are saying in the background, nonetheless, you'll be properly equipped with relevant information about secondary characters and factions. Each line is organically delivered and reinforces each moment's context, mood, and tone.

Negatives of the Narrative

Various missions are repetitive. Their goals are sometimes not meaningful; they are, rather, just another excuse to introduce a new environment with more dangerous confrontations and physical activities. You could easily substitute a Communications Station or Bridge with another locale and not have any bearing on the plot or character development. And the more locations that were added, the more it felt like the game was delaying the achievement of something big and meaningful, story-wise. Obviously, these locales introduce more gameplay opportunities and cool confrontations, but they are hollow by nature because they are just buying time. This is typical of games. The goal is often to be mission-based, not character-based. That's a harsh thing to accept as a storyteller. It is the reality, nonetheless.

Also, the game is very cut-scene heavy. This may not be a bad thing for gamers who love narrative. However, as mentioned several times beforehand, most gamers view cut scenes as interruptions to gameplay. But it just so happens that *these cut scenes are done so well.* If one doesn't like them, then it's a matter of personal taste, not lack of quality.

While the character development of *The Last of Us* is pretty stellar, it's not without its flaws. When Ellie escapes to the ranch after hearing that Joel is leaving her with his brother, you'd expect a deeper sense of hurt from Ellie. But instead, her escape is disingenuous; she wants to be found and Joel does so quickly. She wants a platform to show her pain and castigate him for his skittishness toward her. The moment is emotionally false and contrived. But it's just one false move in an otherwise masterwork of video game narrative.

In Conclusion

The Last of Us is a masterpiece of interactive fiction. It tells a great story, not just for games, but for any medium. The excellence doesn't stop there; it's a fun game to play too. This is unique in the games industry. Seldom does a game meet the quality bar for both narrative and gameplay. Telltale Games were known for their world-class storytelling in games before they closed shop in November 2018. But were the games compelling from a gameplay standpoint? I was fascinated with the choices I made and their downstream effects in the episodes of *The Walking Dead* video game. I would then replay an episode and choose different options to see how distinct the consequences were from the first go-around. The game was interesting and artfully executed, but I can't say that I experienced adrenaline-fueled, maniacal buttoning of the controller. Nor can I say that I had fun. That's the essence of games. In fact, that's the intent. And that's why Naughty Dog is in a class by itself.

CHAPTER 9

Breaking In

B ECAUSE NARRATIVE DESIGN AND game writing are creative endeavors, they face the same ups and downs for employment that musicians, actors, screenwriters, and artists do. Granted, getting a staff job with a publisher mollifies some of that anxiety. However, unless the publisher or studio you're working for is story-centric or has multiple titles that you are tending to, brace yourself for rough waters ahead. Storytellers play second fiddle to pure designers, programmers, and audio engineers. As stated many times before, gameplay is king. If it can live without story, then polish your resume when your company needs to tighten its budget.

Now, this isn't to say you shouldn't pursue game writing or narrative design. It just means to move forward and prepare yourself mentally for a volatile industry. Your first concern should be getting your foot in the door.

ENTRY POINTS

The industry's massive financial growth for nearly fifteen years is due to its increasing global popularity and steady replacement of film as the pop culture go-to. Those who want to make games play games, and since the number of players has increased over the years, it follows that the number of desired game-makers has increased as well.

Assuming you don't have an older sibling that owns a game studio, there are four paths to breaking in:

- *The university path.* Enroll in a college or graduate school that offers degrees in game development and internship opportunities at game studios. There are a growing number of schools that offer these programs including the University of Southern California, Rensselaer Polytechnic Institute; University of Utah; Michigan State University; Full Sail University; University of Central Florida; and Carnegie Mellon University. (I provide a larger list in this book's addendum.)

- *The tester path.* Apply for jobs as a game tester, where your primary responsibility will be playing games, testing them for bugs, and reporting these glitches to the relevant feature owners. (This position is also known as a Quality Assurance Analyst, or QA Analyst.) By starting as a tester, you will work yourself up to a junior position in another department (usually design or engineering) upon which your path to creating content for games begins.

- *The experienced-professional-from-another-field path.* These folks include programmers, artists, writers, project managers, and others. They often make a seamless fit due to their breadth of experience from another field. These professionals offer a different set of skills and perspectives that are helpful in making a product better and innovative.

- *The make-your-own-game path.* If you have money saved up, it might be worth creating and distributing your own game on a mobile device or on Steam, a video game distribution platform run by the Valve Corporation. While this might seem like an expensive endeavor (and it is!), it is an investment for the future. You will be developing a series of transferable skills that is used often in game development. These include project management; producing; designing; writing; marketing; trademark oversight; directing voice-over talent; etc. If you are an outsider and your game is playable, game developers will appreciate your effort. You now have something in common: surviving the back-breaking, overwhelming, and sleepless process known as game development. *Developing the empathy is just as important as adopting the skill-set.*

But no matter your background or experience level, getting hired depends a lot on the "EQ" or emotional quotient you bring to the interview. You will meet people of various backgrounds and expertise who are attempting to get a "feel" for you as a potential co-worker.

Attitude

People in the games industry work extremely long hours. The demands are constant and often are a hybrid of technical and creative challenges.

Using both the left and right brain hemispheres can cause one's focus to be diffuse. So, the last thing a developer wants to deal with is an unnecessary distraction … in the form of a co-worker.

Game professionals are looking to work with those who check the ego at the door, aren't precious over their work, and are flexible and nimble when curveballs are thrown their way (which is basically all the time).

An interview doesn't often reveal these attitudes, at least not in a genuine sense. That's why past work experience and, more importantly, reference checks will confirm (or deny) that the candidate is in possession of the right qualities.

What is often revealed in interviews, however, is the general attitude someone has toward games. This is often a trap for people who come from another industry, many of whom have never picked up a controller before. A holier-than-thou attitude can often emerge; same with the attitude of "Well, my kids play X, therefore I am qualified to tell you how I feel about your product." No.

You will never be hired based on what other people think of games; you will be hired based on what *you* think of games. If you cannot deign to pick up the sticks or if you look at games as a lesser medium (which many prospective candidates do), it is best to look elsewhere for employment. The long hours, the internal product reviews, and the conversations with employees are extremely humbling. Games are constantly in flux, even after content lock (thanks to periodic software updates). This means one has to have an appetite and the intestinal fortitude to muscle through constant criticism, last-minute innovations, and endless technical bugs.

Games are fun to play. Making them, however, can be drudgery.

Familiarity

It's required that a prospective candidate study up (that is, play) the product they are interviewing for. What's more, they ought to have a broad sense of the competition. Candidates will often be asked about what improvements they would bring to the next version of the game they're interviewing for and what innovations they would offer to differentiate it from the competition.

It's also important to be "in the know," so that you can speak to how the game compares to others in its genre and in the industry at large. Innovations from a game in one genre can inspire innovations in another. *Destiny*, for instance, influenced multiple games in numerous genres to adopt hero customization. PlayerUnknown's Battlegrounds, aka PUBG, made their mark on the industry in 2017 by popularizing the multiplayer "battle royale" fighting genre. Soon after, Epic Games saw the potential in it and repurposed a survival game of theirs called *Fortnite* into a cooperative battle royale game. Three billion dollars later (and counting!), *Fortnite* has taken the video game industry by storm and has forced big-time game publishers to create their own battle royale games to stanch hemorrhaging stock prices.

It's also important to come prepared to discuss your craft and how you would leverage it to add value to the game. *As a narrative designer, what will you do to make the story of this franchise better? How will you improve the narrative mechanics so that story is more seamlessly intertwined with gameplay?* So, be ready to discuss games that you've played recently and what you thought were missed opportunities in the storytelling. This will show an interest in the medium as well as a command of your craft.

Lastly, it's important to have experience in certain technologies that will mostly likely be outside of your area of interest. Excel, Jira, Microsoft Project, Visio – all of these are tools that are used frequently in game development shops. Excel, for instance, enables the sharing of story content with other disciplines, who work in nothing but spreadsheets. Jira allows project managers to see how well you are progressing toward major deadlines. These tools might seem counterproductive for a writer, but they are a necessary evil for the betterment of the team. Never forget: *games are a highly collaborative industry.*

Larger Perspective Than Games

As a narrative designer, you will be driving countless brainstorming sessions with creative directors, game designers, artists, and even engineers. It is common for these people to know the medium of games really well, but when pushing these folks to think outside of the industry, you will get the same set of intellectual properties (IPs) thrown at you: *Star Wars, Harry Potter, The Lord of the Rings*, and a superhero movie or two (or 30!).

The pool of resource material is very limited, and as such can be stifling creatively. But these professionals aren't hired to be well rounded in the narrative of other media. Rather, you are! It is important to have a broad exposure to and knowledge of well-told stories in various media. How an author decided to unravel a story beat, no matter the genre, will be instructive for whatever narrative you are trying to map out.

And I cannot say this enough: read books. And read books that are not only sci-fi, fantasy, or horror. Today's game narrative suffers too much from copying the same tropes of the same genre of other games. And if it's not from other games, it's from the same episode of *The Walking Dead* or a short story by HP Lovecraft. Not a bad place to start, but the reading and watching must continue to other destinations – foreign destinations especially (that is, <u>not</u> sci-fi, fantasy, or horror). Be comfortable with reading literature. Homer and Shakespeare offer the clearest and oldest examples of character and story structure, upon which modern day drama (be it television, film, theater, or fiction) is built. Reading non-fiction is perhaps even more important. Real-life legends in history can be inspirations for characters in your narrative. Understanding their psychology and their backstory will fuel your imagination and make your characters' motivations more believable.

IF YOU COME FROM ANOTHER MEDIUM, WHAT SHOULD YOU EXPECT?

Television and film writers often have a hard time making the transition into games mainly because the script in traditional media is sacrosanct. It is the cardinal blueprint of production. True, dialogue gets changed all the time when you're on a film set. But the trajectory of the story (typically) remains intact once the camera rolls. People know what to expect in the next scene.

In the game world, the script (when there is one) does not command that degree of respect. Instead, the central document to which all the stakeholders refer is the GDD or game design document. This is a comprehensive document that provides the creative vision of the game as well as breakdowns for each mode and feature. The GDD is in constant flux, mainly because features in the game either expand or contract based on ongoing industry trends or focus group testing. Once again, the games business is the business of software development. When technologies evolve, this forces everything else to change with it. A game can expand in scope anywhere in its development, in which case new content will need to be created and current content will need to be updated. Conversely, if the technologies contract (due to schedule, personnel, or budget), teams will cut or diminish features and modes. Narrative is often the first to get hit.

A writer from another medium will not be able to survive in this world without being nimble. Changes happen all the time and narrative is not immune. This can be frustrating for traditional screenwriters, who may be accustomed to altering scenes or bits of dialogue, but never wholesale changes of the mechanisms that deliver narrative, such as changing a cutscene into a non-voiced, non-animated branching conversation with an

NPC. This involves a massive amount of work and can seem ludicrous (and often is!), but it is not out of the ordinary. Again, games are software. Tech always comes first.

As mentioned earlier in this chapter, traditional screenwriters will also have to be comfortable with writing in different software that isn't writer friendly. Most of the time, narrative designers and game writers will be writing in a spreadsheet. Microsoft Excel (and, at a growing rate, Google Sheets) provides a wide breadth of data in individual cells that are relevant to different disciplines in game development. As discussed in Chapter #4, a spreadsheet makes it possible to monitor a single line of dialogue throughout the content creation pipeline. With every written line, you will have a corresponding asset ID, which will be the identification signifier that designers and audio engineers use to implement in the game. The Localization team, as well, will use that same asset ID when translating a single line into numerous languages.

Although crucial to the collaborative process, spreadsheets are the most counter-intuitive software for a writer. Filling in a narrow cell with dialogue is a lifeless process. Writing is often about human emotion, and there's nothing farther from emotion than a spreadsheet. Not to mention, it stymies the momentum of the writing process when one must endlessly manipulate the cells to accommodate new collaborators from different disciplines. Game developers often don't relate to this, and it's incredibly frustrating to deal with these constraints day in, day out.

I recommend those not familiar with spreadsheets to write their content in other software (like Word or Final Draft) and then copy and paste their work into the appropriate cells. This is not ideal, but it is par for the course. And it is something writers need to be comfortable with if they wish to pursue this field.

Once again, games are software, and the development of software is not always an organic fit for creatives, who thrive on the open canvas. Software development, on the other hand, has very structured and pronounced confines. To thrive as a writer in this world is to embrace those confines.

CHAPTER 10

Rules and Tools for Success

BECAUSE OF THE INTENSE collaborative nature of games, a narrative designer cannot write without confines. This can be constrictive for those who come from another medium such as film, fiction, or theater where the immediate process of writing is owned and governed by the author. Game narrative is typically a reactive discipline. Ideas often originate from a creative director who sets the vision of the game. This vision will include: the type of game (first person shooter, real-time strategy, platformer, etc.); its premise; the type of experience for players; and the golden path.

Creative directors are also on task to incorporate data and marketplace trends to shape their vision. These business interests can't be ignored. Game companies can invest tens, if not hundreds, of millions of dollars in a single title. The directive that emerges – ala a *Fortnite* copy, or the next futuristic FPS, or a mobile Match 3 game – will be the north star for the creative director.

Writers and narrative designers are often not consulted in this early phase ... and much to the game's detriment. Premise and golden path are, by their nature, so rooted in worlds, characters, and stories that it is only logical that they'd be workshopped with writers. Once again, the game world is a world of software. There are certain processes in place in which content is created. Bringing writers in *after* the vision is created should be a relic of the old school way of game development, but it is not. What can be built, technology-wise, is often the starting point. The creative follows. This is not a universal (nor ideal) process for all game studios, but it is still the most common.

FLEXIBILITY

With that in mind, narrative designers and writers must be okay with contributing after the vision has been cemented and working within confines that may not be narrative-friendly. Not all cool games make for great stories. (That said, not all great stories make for cool games.)

Thus, the first rule of success is flexibility. Realize that when you come to a team, while you are desired for a special skill, you are not a priority ... at first. Game developers will never realize how crucial narrative is until it's in the game, weeks before content lock. Then they will hound you to make improvements until the very last hours before everyone is "pencils down."

During this time, you'll be thrown a ton of change requests that might undermine the narrative. With time ticking away, you'll have to use the limited options in your quickly dwindling arsenal. The revision process will involve: (a) figuring out ways to accommodate those last-minute changes in various narrative mechanisms; (b) identifying their downstream effects on the writing; and (c) writing those narrative fragments in a way that is neither awkward nor excessive so as not to bore or confuse the player.

That's the goal, but then reality sets in. Consider, if you will, an environment that has been cut at the last minute along with a crucial cut scene. A narrative designer will need to redistribute all of its relevant story information to other narrative mechanisms found in other environments in order to maintain story coherence. The information from that cut scene will eventually transform into – wait for it – an inelegant moment of exposition, either through voice-over from in-game dialogue or through UI text.

This is only a hypothetical, but it is similar to the types of compromises one should expect. Few people understand how fragile a story's architecture is. One arbitrary addition to or subtraction from a game feature could potentially cause the narrative structure to collapse. This is a constant challenge for storytellers. Finding ways to sustain the integrity of the story will be a tireless effort amidst the chaos of the game development cycle.

BRAINSTORMING SESSIONS

Once you join a game studio, you will quickly discover that the whiteboard will be your best friend. Ideas will be generated at rapid speed when the team is in the blue-sky phase of product development. Anything goes at this point. The transcribing of ideas, the mapping out of flows, and the prioritizing of creative pillars will decorate the whiteboard. Each brainstorming session will feature a new set of ideas ... and handwriting. The most important contributions from the team are not the amount of ideas, but rather the parameters of the creative vision, which is often in an amorphous, unclear state. Creative directors ought to lead these initial discussions. This could take weeks to cement. Afterwards, the narrative will start to emerge.

The narrative designer's greatest impact will be in organizing the ideas behind each creative pillar as it relates to story. She will draw connections between these ideas and subtly advocate for quality. The latter issue requires that the narrative designer reject ideas that are non-sensical, unachievable, off-brand, and/or downright offensive. She will be the gatekeeper of practicality, common sense, and good taste. She will also need to find the optimal actualization of narrative. If the product, for instance, is a family-oriented Match 3 mobile game, a narrative designer will need to add story within the limited confines of UI text. *Where and how*, she will ask herself? Does each Match 3 victory trigger a fragment of backstory or lore of the fictional universe of the game? After five achievements, does the player receive a letter from their fictional mom saying how proud they are? "If only you could break my record of twenty-five straight wins ..." Corny as that might sound, the player is given a specific goal rooted in a story, mainly about honoring your fictional mother's wishes. A narrative designer must always look for these opportunities and then ask tough questions to the team, such as, "What more can narrative do here?" At this stage, the job is to minimize the amount of missed opportunities for story.

The tough questions and their answers set a strong foundation for the brainstorming sessions. Once those basics are answered, it's then a matter of getting more specific with the narrative and how it works within the different elements of gameplay. The team will look to you to be the subject matter expert on story, and you will need to push back when the gameplay overwhelms or diminishes it. Without these brainstorming sessions, games will be created in silos. Seldom does that make for a fun player experience.

ROBUST DOCUMENTATION

Game developers love documentation. And why not? It provides the blueprint from which game features or systems are created. In addition to the GDD, ancillary design documents will describe features in great detail, and will be shared among all disciplines within the studio. Documentation provides visibility and updates for everyone involved, and will welcome feedback and contributions from members of the development team.

Many writers who join a team for the first time think they have but one goal: to write scripts or on-screen text. But that process is usually *the result of* copious narrative documentation. The following is a list of the types of documentation a narrative designer or game writer will take on before the actual scriptwriting begins.

Story Bible

A writer will often be tasked to write the lore of the world of the game. Their only fodder in the beginning will most likely be a premise, similar to an elevator pitch, which is a clear, concise, and vibrant description of your story's premise. Hook your audience in to something exciting. The goal then is to take the premise and create a mythology that is designed for that game only.

This mythology will include the visual descriptions of the locales of the games; their backstories; the biographies of the primary and secondary characters; an in-depth story summary, beat by beat; and descriptions of the sequels (implying that the game is a franchise and not a one-off).

The latter is important, as it provides a direction beyond the project at hand and will therefore force the writers to plant seeds in the first game that can blossom for each sequel. Remember: blockbuster games are franchises, and you'll always want to be thinking in those terms. (Indie games are the exception, but seldom do indie studios have enough budget (read: money) to support a full-time writer.)

Story bibles are living documents. They evolve as the franchise evolves. Characters and worlds will be added to it. And as the story summaries per each game are added, the bible not only serves as a guide for writers, artists, and programmers, but it also serves as a brand source for marketing teams, book publishers, or film companies who plan to bring your game to life in their respective field(s). Therefore, story bibles should be well organized, up-to-date, and comprehensive.

Crucial Component to Story Bible: Visual Structure

Writers share a common language. Inciting incident, climax, obligatory scene, etc., are structural terms that we toss back and forth to one another as a way to understand or improve the structure of a story. But for those who are outside of the field, it is a challenge to explain what these terms mean.

What I have found most useful is mapping out the structure of a story through a diagram. Structural milestones will be inserted on the graph, as if they were coordinates on a map. Those higher on the graph serve as big, exciting moments or reveals for the story. I then draw a single line that connects these various coordinates together.

There are various reasons behind this exercise that go beyond communicating structure to outsiders. The visual map is an opportunity for writers to see the pacing of structural milestones and to "flip" coordinates or fill in story beats in between coordinates to prevent inactivity of the story.

Figure 4 is an example of a visual graph. There is no one right answer on how to map out your story. Different types of stories dictate their own pacing and milestones. However, there are some basic requirements that need to be on your map. First discussed in Chapter #6, these story milestones are the *bare minimum requirements* for any visual graph. To recap:

Inciting Incident – what is the event that puts the journey of your protagonist in motion?

The Point of No Return – the moment in your story where the character has made a commitment to his/her mission and cannot back out. Doing so would be cowardly or dishonorable. But from a sheer practical standpoint, if the hero regrets their decision and decides to turn back, then the story ends right there.

Midpoint/Low Point – this is the moment in the hero's journey where they have been momentarily defeated. It seems as if the future is grim. If they can get over this hump, they will renew their sense of purpose and come out a stronger hero.

Ticking Time Bomb – the hero must act fast, now that the villain has introduced a new threat. The intensity and tempo of the hero's journey increase exponentially. The stakes are too high for the hero to fail.

Obligatory Scene/Climax – the moment where the hero has solved the most difficult challenge of the entire story and instantly changes the power dynamic of the world around him/her. For example, a nuclear bomb has been launched toward New York; the hero (most likely a superhero, in this case) changes its direction in the nick of time and then disarms the missile before it can explode. The citizens of New York, once terrified for their lives, can now breathe a sigh of relief.

These five story beats provide the necessary escalation of the protagonist's journey and set a course for clear moments that test the hero and

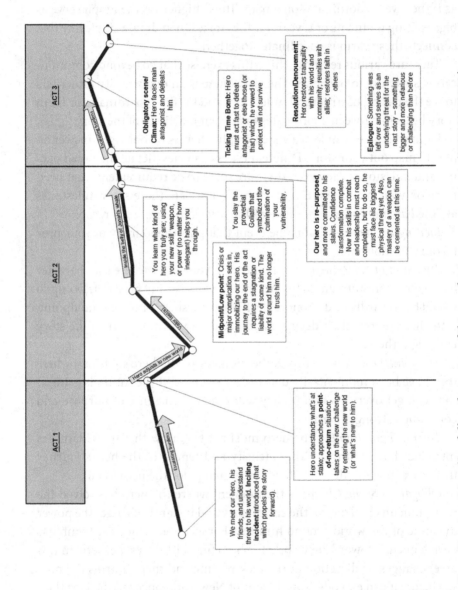

FIGURE 4   Story Structure Map. (See full-scale version of this graph at www.crcpress.com/9781138319738.)

make him/her more compelling. Everything else in between is up to the writer. But to have a solid foundation in the story's structure, the writer must assure that these five story milestones are stakes in the ground, wherein there should be little-to-no adjustment once the story is set.

Granted, changes will always happen. But these milestones should serve as guides toward the completion of the story. If there is something new that develops and causes, for example, the climax to change, this should not cause tremendous disruption where you lose sight of what the story is about. The goal of having immutable (or nearly immutable) stakes in the ground is to force yourself to be creatively disciplined and make strategic decisions that enhance what's already there. If a milestone changes and forces the significant revision of other milestones, it is likely that: (a) that story was not well-thought out to begin with; or (b) you need to change the entire story due to higher business demands or budgetary restrictions.

Always do your best to stay loyal to the strict story pillars you establish early on. Otherwise, there will be no end to the writing. There's too much at stake for you and your fellow game devs. You don't want to be the bottleneck of the content creation pipeline.

Other Components to a Story Bible

Collaboration can be a wonderful thing, but it does have its limits, especially when there are countless opinions from people with no experience in the task at hand. Narrative is a prime target. Everyone has an opinion about it, everyone is quick to judge, and everyone is quick to criticize. And seldom is everyone on the same page.

It's hard to juggle numerous opinions at once. Strike that – *it's impossible*. But what is possible is developing documentation that provides the team with great visibility into the progress of the development of the narrative.

Tone Document

Tone should be one of the first pillars of the creative direction of a game. The senior creative team – which includes, among others, the creative director, executive producer, senior producer, lead designer(s), animation director, and art director – should come up with this pillar in the early days of conception. Tone is a creative driver; it is the common denominator that bonds other parts of game development together. It is also a north star that helps keep in line all of the other creative disciplines such as art, narrative, and sound.

In the *God of War* series, the tone could be described as intense, dark, contemplative, and fierce. In *Legend of Zelda* franchise, the tone is adventurous, dangerous yet optimistic. In *Dead Space*, as with most horror-survival games, the tone is menacing, scary, stressful. In each of those descriptions, the expectation for every creative discipline is to fulfill that tone and infuse it in nearly every part of the creative. At times, other disciplines might look to the narrative designer to help define the tone or at least crystallize it.

One-Pager

Now, while *Call of Duty: Trade War* or *Fortnite Battle Royale for the Elderly* might sound catchy, a pithy idea means nothing if there's no heft behind it. A one-pager will help you communicate a viable premise and the makings of a good story. Told in under a page, this summary will focus less on narrative design and more on marketing. So, use active verbs, avoid long sentences, and keep the language simple.

There will be a ton of iteration on this, not surprisingly. Some might quibble with the premise, while others might argue about the characters. The whole point of this document is to start a conversation. Most folks may be too close to the subject matter to see what they're creating. An outsider, like a game writer or narrative designer, will bring weaknesses to light. By taking a team's callow pieces and putting them together (after adding a dose of coherence and writerly flare, of course), the narrative designer will provide an unvarnished premise of the game. It's then up to the creative leadership to optimize for success.

Elevator Pitch

This was discussed in the section "ID the IP" in Chapter #3. As a reminder: you'll need to provide a basic description of the story in 40–50 words in no more than 2–3 sentences. It can be part of the one-pager or live separately. I recommend opening your one-pager or intro to the story bible with an elevator pitch. It gives a strong and clear message as to what the story is. Your goal is to write something easily understood and compelling while setting the tone.

Take once again, *The Last of Us*: After a pandemic causes infected humans to destroy the rest of civilization, a survivor is hired to smuggle a young teenage girl out of an oppressive military quarantine. Their brutal journey across the country forces them to redefine their relationship to the world and to each other.*

Clear, exciting, dangerous – that's a great takeaway. This elevator pitch may not tell the entire story of the game, but it tells enough. It describes something that people will want to play.

The movie industry has been doing this successfully for years. They've even developed a shorthand for popular movies that piggyback on previous blockbusters.

Die Hard on a ship = *Under Siege*

Lethal Weapon meets martial arts = *Rush Hour*

Toy Story under water = *Finding Nemo*

Breakfast Club meets vampires = *Twilight*

This shorthand technique is not something I would necessarily include in your elevator pitch. Perhaps it's a sentence within the body of the one-pager, used to reinforce a larger point. What's important is for the author to ask themselves, *How can I get people excited about this project and let them know it's a blockbuster in the making?* That answer will dictate the elevator pitch.

Character Bios and Sample Dialogue

Another crucial document that you should prioritize is character biographies. What are their backstories and affiliations? What's their psychological makeup? How do they communicate through sample dialogue? The goal here is to establish an agreed-upon voice of the characters. Creative directors, designers, artists, and others will need to reach consensus in order to assure that the tone of the characters' voices is consistent with the tone of their work.

It is also extremely helpful to write sample dialogue so that the creative leads can determine whom they will want to cast for those characters (assuming the game has a budget for cut scenes or other voice-over opportunities). Characters aren't just created when you play them for the first time. They have a past, and that past often informs their personality, their linguistic style, their decisions, their friendships, and their rivalries.

---

* ("The Last of Us" 2013)

A good writer doesn't just make up those moments on the fly. One must put serious thought into how these characters came to be.

Genre and Platform

Is the game a first-person shooter for PS4 and Xbox One? Or a point-and-click mystery for the PC? Tell the reader what kind of game it is and on what platform(s) a consumer will play it.

Backstory of the World

The environment that a player finds herself in must be designed intricately. After all, without a visually interesting world, why play it? Every environment reflects the tone of the story and can hint at its past. When playing *Fallout 4*, for example, you see a barren wasteland with abandoned buildings and vehicles. How did this world become post-apocalyptic?

As mentioned in Chapter #5, the environment or world is a character unto itself. It has a past, a personality, and a purpose. What happened there before the game began should inform the current plot. If the land was decimated by an evil force, it's likely that that force will re-appear and your protagonist will have to confront him/her.

If the environment is futuristic and hi-tech, how does your protagonist relate to this world? What is their role here? And what drove this world to its current state?

If the environment is a moment in history – like the American West of the early 1900s (*Red Dead Redemption*) or Ancient Egypt (*Assassin's Creed Origins*) – is your character a significant part of it? Or, are there well-known historical events that happened before the start of the game that your character was directly affected by?

The backstory of the world is crucial to establish. It not only affects the characters in the game, but also gameplay events and visual and audio cues that add specificity (and, at times, authenticity) to the world. Your description will not only inform the narrative, but will also assist artists, audio engineers, level designers, and gameplay designers to do their best work.

PRODUCTIVITY AND VISIBILITY TOOLS

Strict milestones dictate the development of the game. These milestones include (but are not limited to) pre-production, production, and alpha (the final stage in which content is inserted into the game).

Within each of these milestones, there are sprints where teams commit to the creation or development of specific deliverables within a brief time frame. This is a very tech-centric process devoted to tracking progress (through an agile planning tool like Jira) and supervised by a project manager or producer. Writers and narrative designers live within a nebulous world of sprints. Tracking the writer's work doesn't smoothly correspond to tracking the work of a programmer or game designer. Narrative is often not a driver of a feature that involves serious technical requirements. Narrative can inspire the creation of features. But once the basics of the feature are articulated, a pure designer takes it from there and works with engineers to build it. Once the shell of the feature is coded, narrative designers and writers will then fill in that shell with content.

Writers and narrative designers must: (a) determine the dates by which the "tranches" of content are expected for delivery; and (b) map out those deliverables to the sprints.

Writers can work in isolation; however, as long as they are organized and in constant communication with other collaborators, deliverables will be accomplished on-time. But team members aren't accountable only to one another. Director-level staff need to have visibility into each person's progress, so that they can determine where help is needed and where budgets can expand.

Moreover, there are people outside of your team that may not work with you on a daily basis, but could have a secondary connection to you. They will need to check in on your progress to see if there is anything that might block them in the near future. Motion Capture studio managers have very strict deadlines. If they know you are writing a cut scene, they will need to know when it is due so that they can adjust their schedule to film it. It is likely they are accommodating multiple games within the same company.

If the sprint process is too difficult to adopt, you can ease into it by setting up an editorial calendar and filling it with specific due dates for deliverables. Using Outlook Calendar is a great tool for this. However, you'll need to transpose those weekly or daily tasks into task-management tracking software, like Jira or Asana, so that project managers know what you're up to. In this day and age, tech professionals cannot avoid agile planning software.

For brainstorming and mapping out high-level structure, diagramming software is the perfect tool. It provides a clear, visual representation of a story flow. Once story milestones are set, you'll map out of the sequence of events in Visio, OmniGraffle, or Gliffy only to discover what works, what is missing, and what needs to get fixed.

For presentations – of which there will be a countless number – PowerPoint and Keynote remain the industry standard. Everyone in a development team will have to make internal presentations at least a few times in a dev cycle. Building a deck with compelling images is practically required these days. So, if you're someone who's just comfortable with writing words, make sure to team up with a visual professional to make your presentations compelling. This is crucial. Most of a narrative designer's work *will not be read until the end of the dev cycle* where the quality assurance team is hard at work, making sure there are no flaws in the writing or in its execution. A clear-cut, visual pitch will mobilize the support you need from leadership early on in the dev cycle.

Finally, as discussed earlier, proficiency in Excel or Google Sheets goes a long way when writing dialogue. Not only is the spreadsheet the most effective data input tool, but it is also the perfect centralized hub for different disciplines to work from and track the implementation history of each line of dialogue or on-screen text.

CHAPTER 11

Present Day Demands and Challenges

FRICTIONLESS NARRATIVE

A major challenge for narrative designers today is how to present the story without interrupting the gameplay. The appetite for narrative varies from consumer to consumer. But it is often the case that gamers do not want their gaming sessions to be halted or distracted in any way. Distractions include bugs or software glitches, unnecessary grinding missions, and even annoying music. Narrative is often seen as a distraction as well. A lot of gamers feel that if they wanted to have a story, they'd watch a movie.

Yet, narrative is beloved by many. And the industry often embraces narrative as a baseline requirement for a solid score on the game review aggregation website known as *Metacritic*. It is so influential, in fact, that a studio will hire former reviewers to play-test an upcoming game solely to predict its *Metacritic* score. (As a result, the dev team will make last-minute, targeted improvements on certain features and/or change its marketing strategy.)

How narrative integrates with gameplay is something that narrative designers solve for every day. Stopping the gameplay for a cut scene is too disruptive, as it prevents the player from interacting with their screen. In-game dialogue is better, but not perfect. This involves a player to enter a new environment and interact with NPCs. They will gradually reveal, through voice-over or on-screen text, the mysteries of the environment or share with you crucial information that could influence decisions you make in the future. Being overloaded with information is not ideal for most gamers, who just want to zone out and play. Nonetheless, in-game dialogue is often a successful alternative to the cut scene.

Then there are discoverable items – for example, The Riddler's letters in *Batman: Arkham Asylum* or the radio recordings or voxophones in *BioShock* and *BioShock: Infinite*, respectively – that can be read or listened to at a player's own pace after they are collected. They can be saved in your inventory of items or can be instantly activated once collected. Discoverable items, or collectibles, are a way to steadily deliver bits of the narrative without much friction. There is a flipside, however. If these story bits offer too much content per collection and/or require frequent collection, a player will reach narrative fatigue and stop absorbing the story. A player will likely avoid collecting further, especially if it has no bearing on the gameplay.

Then there is the conversation tree mechanic, which we discussed in Chapter #7. As a refresher: when an NPC asks a player a question, the player will have one of two (if not more) choices to select from. The outcome of the conversation could lead to a different story path or provide slightly altered content based on the attitude you just gave in your responses. The results of these decisions form dialogue trees. They're called that because paths can "branch," or form a new direction, based on one's decisions.

If there is neither an influence on the gameplay nor a slight modification on the narrative, then the dialogue is meaningless. The narrative should be designed in a way where it has consequences on the gameplay or can be modified through decision points. At the very least, the conversation should reward a player with a gift (like a weapon or experience points). But a different outcome of the player's journey should be the prime ambition.

One could argue that an ideal frictionless narrative is one that is not on the same screen as the game. The concept of the second-screen experience has been experimented with over the last decade. It is not designated to games only.

In 2012, Disney released the Blu-ray of the sci-fi adventure film *John Carter,* an adaptation of the Edgar Rice Burroughs' novels. The film production was massive in budget (over $250 million, not including $100 million for marketing) and failed to make a profit. While subsequent plans for a sequel were quashed, the home entertainment experience, however, flourished.*,†

---

* ("John Carter of Mars" 2012)
† (Strowbridge 2012)

One could attribute such success – $19.3 million in home entertainment sales in its opening weekend; $38 million overall – to the innovative features it offered, including the (then) recently anointed *Disney Second Screen* experience. Through the use of a smartphone or tablet app, a consumer could watch the film and receive supplemental content through one's device. For example, audio cues in the film would get triggered by the app when the customer read a journal entry written by the protagonist. The journal also offered interactive character art that consumers could manipulate and gain further context into the *John Carter* universe.

Games are the perfect medium for this and have already-explored second-screen possibilities. The widely popular first-person shooter *Destiny* offers Grimoire cards for players to read on the internet. Unlocked with every milestone achievement, each card would reveal the lore of the world and the characters who live in it.

Migrating to another technology (in this case, from console to computer) provided seamless enjoyment in the *Destiny* experience. A player had the freedom to absorb the narrative whenever they saw fit without interrupting their gameplay.

Second-screen experiences were more popular from 2012 to 2014 than they are as of this writing. Today, many games have a companion app that is not critical to experiencing the game; however, it enhances one's gaming experience either by providing reward opportunities, navigational assistance, or reminders to upcoming events in the game. Basically, companion apps are rebranded second-screen experiences.

How do we explain the staid enthusiasm for second-screen experiences? This is the natural evolution of product and feature development. Companies hope that people will break old habits or loyalties to adopt new ones. When the product comes out, there is an initial wave of excitement. People experiment with it and often have a positive reaction. Alas, there is no follow-through, especially if the product has no utility outside of entertainment. Today's slow adoption of virtual reality might shed light on why second-screen experiences did not take off like they should have. People fear change. They like what they have and can only absorb something new in small bits before the appetite increases at a snail's pace or vanishes entirely. By then, the product is no longer in the conversation.

It is also possible that the second-screen experience, in general, was not designed as well as it could have been. What's the incentive for a player to leave one platform for the next, even if the departure is momentary? Is there something they can gain that is meaningful and neither contrived, manipulative, nor distracting? Also, if the second-screen experience must happen simultaneously while playing the game, is that too much pressure to put on a player? Is it over-stimulating? Perhaps this is why Grimoire cards, which can be experienced upon one's convenience, is a more successful example.

Yet what if Grimoire cards were not only a result of a gameplay unlock, but also could affect gameplay? Perhaps it would drive more players to the computer to check them out. Or perhaps it is as simple as offering a narrative experience vs. a non-narrative experience on a game's Start Menu. Players can opt in to a "story mode" experience, play the normal golden path of the game, and consume the narrative on another device. If it is branded honestly and clearly from the beginning, it is possible that players will feel respected. They can then play the game a second time but through the mode they opted out of initially.

In the games industry, preserving the consumer goodwill is paramount. If a developer looks like they are not respecting a player's time, there will be severe consequences, from incessant trolling of a company on social media to widespread boycotting of a game's release. More importantly, preserving consumer goodwill by developers comes from a genuine place: *developers are gamers too.*

How did second-screen experiences emerge in the first place? Quite simply, the mobile revolution. When the iPhone premiered in 2007, the technology quickly became less of a telecommunications device and more of a mini-computer. Multi-tasking became commonplace. Fast forward to today: when watching television, consumers have evolved from looking up information about an actor on their phone's browser to communicating with strangers over Twitter or Snapchat about the latest battle in *Game of Thrones.* Concurrent multi-media consumption is the true second-screen experience and has become the new path forward. Therefore, those who design and produce entertainment experiences for this new path will flourish if they can harness the media consumption patterns of today's multi-tasker. It is then only a matter of time when traditional Hollywood entertainment becomes a thing of the past.

Activision-Blizzard, creators of the *World of Warcraft* franchise, have explored a different and very successful approach to frictionless narrative. For their extremely popular multi-player first person shooter (FPS) *Overwatch*, the narrative is explored in comics and animated shorts that are outside of the gameplay. This approach is not a second-screen experience; it is instead a separate media experience with high production values that could be consumed even if you don't play the game. In other words, these story bits are not triggered based on gameplay milestones or achievements. They are instead introduced to the player on a separate release schedule and broaden the fictional universe of *Overwatch* by telling the stories of its various characters. The narrative is not necessary for the gaming experience, but it is rich enough for players to increase their enjoyment of the IP and gain a deeper understanding of its universe and characters.

As gameplay in general becomes more compelling and addictive, narrative will need to become more frictionless. How to tell the narrative will need to be just as innovative as the software behind it. It will be interesting to see if *Overwatch's* external narrative extensions can have evergreen success. If so, it may hold the formula for the future of game narrative.

THE FORTNITE EFFECT

If you've picked up this book, it's likely you've heard of *Fortnite*. The Epic Games smash hit was originally a survival game with unimpressive sales. With the success of PUBG, *Fortnite* followed in its footsteps by building a battle royale mode of their own. The rest is history.

Fortnite has become not only a billion-dollar phenomenon; it has devastated the console games market. *Fortnite* players can seamlessly play across their phones, tablets, and PCs. Console games, on the other hand, restrict players to a single technology. What's more, *Fortnite* is free-to-play (excluding microtransactions), empowers people to play with their friends, and has a vibrant art style and addictive game design. All of these factors have contributed to a dawn of reckoning for major publishers like Electronic Arts, Activision, Take-Two, and Microsoft. Their game sales and stock prices diminished significantly in the second half of 2018. With this massive disruption, one has to ask: Are console games still relevant? Will these publishers have to copy *Fortnite* to survive? Will Google's new streaming service Stadia be another forcing function to change the way games are made and distributed?

Fortnite has no story. It has live in-game events, and people share their gameplay of those events on social media. Followers comment on their gameplay, thus creating a story – or more like news – about that player. This relationship between games and social media has redefined the gaming experience. Players want to show off what they they're doing and get instantaneous replies on Twitter or Twitch. This is nothing new; however, *Fortnite's* fanbase has accelerated this process exponentially.

This fanbase has no time for story. Nor do they have a desire for it. The more they occupy their free time with this game, the less exposure they will have to traditional storytelling. Games, while not a narrative medium primarily, are the last bastion of storytelling for a new generation. In general, just a small percentage of games have narrative. This percentage will continue to shrink the more popular *Fortnite* becomes.

Is this just a trend? Not sure. But the future of interactive storytelling is changing. The answer to its survival might be held outside of games. The rise of podcasts, voice technology (like Alexa or Siri), and "choose your adventure" television (such as *Black Mirror: Bandersnatch*) are promising avenues for storytellers. They also offer a more diverse base of consumers, many of whom are more enthusiastic about storytelling than the average gamer is.

Narrative designers and game writers must view this moment as if it were 1927. The first talking motion picture – *The Jazz Singer* – sent a shockwave through the film industry that forced it to change overnight. Silent movies evaporated in a couple of years. The "scenario writers" who wrote them found themselves out of a job, with nowhere to go. Strong dialogue was in demand. Hollywood came knocking on the doors of New York playwrights to fill that void.

Will we face a similar demise as the scenario writer? Who knows? But the writing is on the wall: to survive is to pivot. There's no better advice I could give than to expand your storytelling tool-set.

CHAPTER 12

The Future of Narrative Design

INTERACTIVE TELEVISION AS GAMES?

Because game narrative is mostly a reaction to gameplay, the future of game storytelling depends on gameplay innovation. It is likely that story will remain a secondary focus for most games. But as games become more integrated with mass culture, will there be an expectation that some games will have to be less interactive and more story-driven in order to appeal to a wider audience?

Or, will interactive TV shows like *Black Mirror: Bandersnatch* be that bridge between interactive entertainment and non-gamers? If so, then is it possible that choosing your own adventure in an episode of television can be classified as a gaming experience?

If the intention of the medium is to tell a story and there are no other typical gameplay mechanics like cooperative play, collection, or puzzle solving, then interactive television is not a game. If there is no reward for choosing a right answer (or a penalty for choosing the wrong one) in an interactive conversation, then it is not a game. If the participant doesn't achieve a clear victory state or sense of achievement at the end of an episode, then it is not a game.

But will these criteria hold true when more people participate? Especially if these new people want something different than what traditional board games and video games have to offer? No. Absolutely not. Games are games. Interactive television is television.

That said, we are living in a highly gamified culture. Game mechanics – like leveling up, earning badges, customizing content based on decisions – have infiltrated business, education, and even health (Fitbit, anyone?). Hotels gamify loyalty programs. Financial service companies leverage chatbots through a very primitive form of branching conversation trees. By leveraging the arcade redemption game mechanic, airlines entice customers to pay for hotel rooms with frequent flyer miles that they achieved over time. So, while there are distinct lines between what is a game and what is interactive entertainment, one cannot deny that the influence of games is everywhere in today's society.

THE RISE OF ESPORTS

eSports (or competitive gaming) is trending significantly and changing spectator sports as we know it. Games like *Fortnite, League of Legends*, and *Dota 2* are captivating millions of fans across the world, who just watch people play video games over Twitch, YouTube, or in person at competitive tournaments. If you didn't catch that, *millions of people are watching people play video games.* This is a new world.

None of these titles, however, features any narrative during the competition. Why? Because audiences do not have the patience for it at that moment. They want to see players compete. Therefore, with the growing popularity of eSports, is there a place for storytelling in the future? Yes, but not in the traditional sense. Narrative designers and game writers will need to adopt craftier ways to drip feed story throughout a game as frictionless as possible. Does one cut out the narrative entirely from the game and reserve it for another medium, like animation or comics, similar to what *Overwatch* does? Or will it come through as constant in-game dialogue enhanced by on-screen UI text? Sure, but will the story be absorbed when it's competing with so much activity?

One needs to look to social media to understand the player's threshold for words and ideas. It all boils down to bite-sized information that is sent out frequently. A standard game narrative will one day be fractured into micro-episodes or story flashes – no more than 30 seconds of a cut scene, no more than a 5-second splash of UI text, or no more than a 30-second interactive conversation.

Rapidly shrinking attention spans are re-defining fun. Game creators must keep players happy by keeping them constantly active. The cut scene, a former narrative driver, has lost its luster. Narrative designers cannot rely on that to tell their stories entirely – or, in most cases, at all. Nor can they view themselves as screenwriters anymore. We are content designers and interactive designers who specialize in a game feature known as story. Due to this sea change, we must abide by this warning: Never do you want a gamer to "lean back" (passive) in a "lean forward" (active) experience.

FUTURE JOB REQUIREMENTS OF A NARRATIVE DESIGNER

Adopting Technical Skills

Companies are going to require my technical responsibilities from narrative designers. If job postings in the last year are any indication, narrative designers are expected these days to implement the narrative vehicles in-game. Requirements that have popped up include "... fluency in one or more scripting languages" or "adding game-like interaction to narratives" (whatever that means). Some related roles that have popped up include Narrative Technical Designer and Narrative Implementer. Both roles require the employee to implement anything related to narrative content in the game in coordination with other technical dependencies.

It bears repeating: games are software. And as software becomes more expansive for the consumer, so too will the challenges for the developer. Will a pure creative role like a narrative designer become a hybrid role: half creative, half technical? The proportions are definitely shifting in the favor of technical know-how. Thus, it doesn't hurt to master one's storytelling chops as well as adopt supplemental technical knowledge to actualize them. Some technical skills include familiarity with JavaScript, Lua, and Python. And, of course, spreadsheet mastery can never be appreciated enough.

Creating a Narrative Tool-Set

The gaming experience has quickly evolved from a solitary experience to a social one. Consoles connected to Wi-Fi enable millions of players across the world to play with or against one another in real-time missions. This cooperative play (aka "co-op") has brought gaming culture to a whole other level. The rise of Twitch – Amazon's streaming platform where people broadcast their live play on an online personalized channel – rewards the co-op experience with exposure to (potentially) millions of channel subscribers across the world. When players are not on Twitch, they are sharing their recorded gameplay moments on YouTube in the hopes of getting enough subscribers to increase ad revenue and to become a social media influencer – an entity that has enough social media clout and exposure to attract brand deals. If a player opts out of the social media influencer path, he/she is nonetheless sharing their gaming experiences through screen-shots or video clips on all social media platforms. The result is a continuous conversation with like-minded players across the world.

Players are creating their own "stories" these days. Story in this case isn't anywhere near what this book has discussed. In the context of social media, a player views story as, essentially, news about themselves. *What feats have I accomplished today that would generate attention from friends and strangers?* These events are personal and attention-getting (and bor-derline exploitative), and can be so powerful a force that traditional story wanes in comparison.

As the marriage between gaming and social media continues to grow, narrative designers face an unpleasant reality: *will I have a place in this industry if this trend continues?* People crave story, be it their own or one that is created by another. That demand will never end. But the 3-act structure? Or well-crafted episodic storytelling ala *Breaking Bad*? Rigor is missing from current social media content creators. Can the trend reverse? Unlikely if game publishers and studios encourage and empower the status quo. They will jump at the chance to integrate a tighter connec-tion between gaming and social media year after year. And they'll redi-rect funds from parts of the game's budget to funnel into this marriage. Narrative will be the first to be affected by this because, as mentioned in the "Frictionless Narrative" section in Chapter #11, anything that is per-ceived as an obstacle to a player's experience is the first to get cut.

Additionally, narrative designers will have to contend with the indus-try's re-definition of story. The term has been co-opted and warped by marketers and brands in the tech industry for nearly a decade. Appealing to a consumer as a storyteller or emphasizing the importance of a con-sumer's "personal story" is just a cheap ploy to lure people into buying or using the products and services of a brand. Social media companies are particularly guilty of this: *Instagram Stories* is a perfect example. But sto-ries aren't being generated here. Stimuli is a better word for it.

Nonetheless, social media platforms are empowering consumers to become creative artists. Many now offer video production tools that were once inaccessible to the average person. People couldn't film themselves before the advent of the smartphone unless they bought a camcorder. Posting it without horribly compressing the file was tremendously dif-ficult until YouTube came around. You soon could get an instant audi-ence by sharing a link of your YouTube video on Facebook. Facebook Live then became a free live streaming service, where you can engage with fans while you're filming.

This is Do It Yourself (DIY) filmmaking at its finest with little-to-no cost for the average person. As long as you have your own mobile phone, Facebook, Twitter, Snapchat, YouTube, and others provide users with a tool-set to be their own filmmaker, celebrity, and storyteller. Games will eventually do the same. The act of creating a game will take longer to develop, but creating a customized conversation about a single player at any given time is the future. To a lesser extent, games are already empowering their players to be light game designers. Many games, like the *FIFA* and *Anthem* franchises, give players basic tools to customize their heroes, be it how they look or what their strengths or powers are. A player will then record their gameplay and share it on social media, showcasing their character with a self-designed, signature artistic style. Players can also customize entire environments!

This is a huge opportunity for narrative designers. While it flies in the face of what pure storytelling is meant to be, we nonetheless will survive if we own this space. What tools can we design for our players that empower their experience and make them a creator? What are all the elements of a gaming experience and how do we tie them together? What curation tools can we create that allow players to enhance their power of engagement with others on social media? But the main question is: *What is story to them and how do we let them tell it?* There is no right answer, obviously; however, we cannot fool ourselves into thinking that narrative design can remain rigid in an effort to stay pure to its roots. Our work may become less about the writing and more about the designing of templates for others to tell stories the way they see fit.

CHAPTER 13

Transmedia

THE CHANGING MEDIA LANDSCAPE

I'll define transmedia in just a bit. Let me first explain why the effort induces an immediate headache. It's not that its definition can't be easily explained; rather, it's just that those who matter most are not receptive to it. And when I refer to "those who matter most," I mean entertainment professionals with access to capital and production infrastructure. These are Hollywood executives stuck in the '90s, who think they're the only game in town when it comes to entertainment. They are people too wrapped up in traditional media and don't see the signs of its demise or, at least, its imminent and radical transformation. This small thinking is definitely a sign of profound arrogance. "Nothing can take away our grip on the world's culture! We own it!" is a common sentiment. Yet, they have no explanation on how game sales have continually eclipsed movie box office revenue for over ten years now.[*][†] It's true that Hollywood still holds the monopoly of glamour and access to bigger stars than those in the digital world or games do. That is destined to change, however.

In 2014, a survey[‡] conducted by Variety Magazine discovered that young millennials and older Gen Z'ers are more familiar with stars on YouTube than stars on television or film. This revelation shook the industry. It was a tell-tale sign that traditional entertainment no longer has a stronghold on pop culture. Entertainment is changing, and Hollywood is falling behind.

---

[*] (Chatfield 2009)
[†] (Shieber 2019)
[‡] (Ault 2014)

The biggest reason for this change is easy access to media through mobile phones. Netflix, Amazon Prime, and Hulu offer great apps that can be consumed through phone, tablet, or streaming device, making it easy to binge-watch your favorite show anywhere – in bed; at a dentist's office; in traffic (if you're a passenger); airport, you name it.

Digital content, however, is not just TV shows reformatted for a different device. Digital content also refers to original content that appears initially on platforms like YouTube and Vimeo and is tailored to the consumption patterns of its viewers. The length of the videos could range from seconds to hours, but they are usually 3–5 minutes long. They could be produced by major brands like Vice Media, AwesomenessTV, or Machinima (may they rest in peace) – each offering original, exclusive content online.* Or, they could come from individuals like Issa Rae ("Awkward Black Girl" "Insecure"), Abbi Jacobson and Ilana Glazer ("Broad City"), or Ben Sinclair and Katja Blichfeld ("High Maintenance"), who created successful shows on YouTube that eventually were adapted into TV shows for HBO and Comedy Central. Amateurs also create their own episodes with varying degrees of success. Those who do well are known as social media influencers and are effective conduits for brands trying to reach larger audiences.

The appeal of digital content is a combination of: bite-sized length; no interruptions from commercials; casual production values (if any, for most shows); specialized content (e.g., subject matter or genre); and continuous output not restricted or dictated by network hiatuses.

There's one more critical element: access to the creators. Often, a creator of a series, especially if it's non-fiction (for example, home repairs or dog rescue), will respond directly to viewers and subscribers to their channel in the comments section under their videos. Also, if they have a website or social media presence, it is not uncommon for these content creators to directly engage in dialogue with fans. It is these social media tools that allow the shows to endure. The more subscribers a show attracts to its YouTube channel, the more ad revenue the creators share with Google (YouTube's parent company). Social media channels are the critical connective tissue that allows fan engagement to thrive.

For all these reasons, digital content is a powerful medium. It listens to the viewer and can directly respond to them, thereby making the content-viewing experience relatable.

---

* Shows that are created specifically for digital platforms like Hulu and Netflix are excluded from this category. Their content is closely aligned to the formats of cable and network shows.

While fan engagement isn't a necessary factor in a transmedia experience, it is a compelling one. And if the creators of the show can respond to fans in the voice of their characters, then it's even more compelling. It potentially gives an audience member investment in the franchise. Could an exchange with a fan be part of the fictional canon of the IP? Could a fan's suggestion influence the next installment of a show? It's possible (barring legal restrictions, of course). Voting for your favorite contestant on *American Idol* or *Dancing with the Stars* is fan participation at its simplest form. Fans can shape future developments of a series by voting for who stays on the show and who gets kicked off. But actual plot points? Shows like *Psych* and the remake of *Hawaii Five-O* have asked fans to vote for an ending of an episode. But are these gimmicks or are they meaningful transmedia storytelling moments?

The traditional Hollywood types would define them as gimmicks. Although they wouldn't be wrong, they'll be short-sighted if they remain complacent. Gimmicks will never innovate how stories can be told. Younger audiences demand more. They consume media on different devices while multi-tasking. They are constantly plugged into what's going on with their favorite shows and its cast through social media. They'll play games as they wait for their next show to stream. Millennials and Gen Z'ers have radically re-set the media landscape in terms of expectations. The traditional entertainment model does not work for them. Transmedia, however, does.

TRANSMEDIA AT ITS MOST BASIC LEVEL

Transmedia, at its purest level, is the communication of a single-story experience* across various, different media. To be clear: this isn't across different parts within a single medium (such as 22 episodes of a season of a single television show). Rather, it is across different *deliverers of media* such as television, books, digital content, games, film, and live events where upon each deliverer provides a different section of that single-story experience. (My *Matrix* graph in the pages that follow demonstrates this in detail.)

This requires a storyteller to designate specific fragments of the story to specific media deliverers and then customize those fragments to the

---

* Story, in this case, is one hero's journey that is either finite or persistent. The focus is on their life and how they react to actions by other characters or events in their world. I delve into another type of transmedia experience that is "less" pure but more common, under the section "Fractured Experience about the World."

grammar of the respective media deliverer. *Why*, you might ask? An episode of television has different rules of storytelling than does a 3-minute video, a feature-length film, or a comic book. To defy those rules is to break each medium's authenticity.

A consumer engages with a specific medium to fulfill certain expectations. A podcast cannot communicate a combat scene as well as a graphic novel can. Yet, an actor's voice from a podcast can be a tonal force that makes characters on a page feel alive and familiar, something that would be lost if a consumer were to read the dialogue in a graphic novel. A big-blockbuster film might be able to check off both boxes of character performance and visual spectacle, but if a consumer wants to control the pacing of the action, they'll read a comic and flip the pages at their own speed.

Relationship with New Technology

Transmedia is a byproduct of tools that allow for communication. These tools – be they smartphones, televisions, radio, movie screens, online forums, live forums – are constantly innovating. This too is a byproduct, but of *how* people communicate.

Does anyone remember Friendster? Or MySpace? These were the social media precursors to Facebook and offered similar functionality, such as emails and public posts among friends. They were a distant (and laughable) memory by the time the mobile revolution hit in 2007. Facebook flourished, nearly a year after it opened its doors to a world outside of the college arena to anyone 13 years and older. As the mobile revolution evolved in the next few years, so did social media. In addition to Facebook, Twitter, Pinterest, Reddit, Snapchat and Instagram (also owned by Facebook) have become the primary media for millions of people around the world and have permanently re-shaped the way people communicate with each other. Now emojis are common replacements for written words, as are pics and video as well.

One could argue that the mobile revolution is still sprinting along while newer technologies, such as Virtual Reality (VR) and Augmented Reality (AR), struggle for mass adoption. With each of these new platforms, there are different rules of communication ... or rather different ways to communicate that are adopted organically and not imposed by the creator(s) of the platform.

Transmedia storytelling reflects – and even mimics – these organic rule-sets because it is doing what good storytelling often does: it promotes the authenticity of a platform. In other words, you're not (likely) going to be writing a two-person script in 140 characters through a single Twitter handle. That example is more appropriate for a play, TV episode, or film. But Twitter is very much capable of delivering drama. Imagine a fictional couple "talking" on Twitter through two different accounts, where dialogue is started by one of the characters and then replied to by the other. The dialogue escalates into an argument about the man's recent flirtation with a co-worker. Insults and revelations of backstory start piling up on a single tweet thread. Each person rotates by offering a new a reply to the other. Soon, followers of these accounts start chiming in. The drama becomes shared, as followers (who are real, mind you) take sides. These followers are not playing fictional characters; they are, instead, interacting with the fiction *as if it were a real part of their lives*. It is now an all-out social media war that was once a catty fictional drama between two lovers. Real people are involved now. They are adding to the fiction, if not through plot points then through enhancement of the tone and mood of this exchange. This "drama" may not be delivered by actors in three acts, but it is just as thrilling and exciting on a new medium that has its own grammar.

But this dramatic moment is not yet transmedia storytelling until the drama spreads to other platforms. So, imagine if one of the fictional characters decides to have a private conversation with followers on Instagram, even posting pictures of his disgruntled yet handsome self. He is unintentionally drawing affection from some of his female followers. They send him overtures of love and even request that he break up with his Twitter girlfriend.

The girlfriend finds out on Instagram what's going on and confronts the boyfriend on Snapchat. The video catches the boyfriend by surprise. Offended by the girlfriend's distrust, he escapes from the camera and takes to Twitter to announce to his followers that he is breaking up with her. Mind you, his break-up tweet is the actual break up, a live announcement that is news to everyone … including the girlfriend!

This "simple" drama unfolded, escalated, devolved, and exploded in three different, but related platforms: Twitter, Instagram, Snapchat. The fact that the drama migrated from one platform to the next is just enough to qualify as transmedia storytelling. (And the cheapest form too!) Going from one social media platform to the next is the bare minimum, as the experience of each of these media is virtually the same: bite-sized info communicated over a short, but intense amount of time; fan participation capabilities; and mobile phone content creation (aka lower production values). The technology for each of these outlets varies slightly, so the content will vary slightly as well. But transmedia storytelling should aim for something more ambitious, where the rule-sets of each medium differ significantly from one to the other. This maximizes the unique affordances of each medium and prevents stagnation of the story.

When Bigger Budgets Prevail

Big-entertainment companies have the financial resources to pull off a compelling transmedia campaign. But they often fail to do anything more than a superficial marketing campaign with zero canonical tie-ins. Ideally, a huge tent pole product (such as a movie or video game) will have a series of transmedia extensions that surrounds its release.

But if the franchise has a series of tent-poles that will be released in a couple of years of one another, a transmedia media extension could fill in the gaps to retain the fanbase and pique their interest with new canonical stories. The transmedia extensions could be anything from a comic series that continues where the video game left off or a series of web shorts that builds up to the opening of a blockbuster film by providing backstory to the fictional universe. More about this later on.

There are a few ambitious examples that have designed the transmedia campaign well in advance and have designated a certain part of that fictional universe to be conveyed through a certain medium. In between each tentpole was significant transmedia "connective tissue" to feed the fanbase. The best example of this is *The Matrix*.

Filmmakers Lana and Lilly Wachowski had a specific story experience in mind when they first conceived of the franchise. Its fictional universe was so vast that one film would not suffice in telling the entire lore. After the success of the first film, the Wachowskis decided to continue the story across different media touchpoints that, ultimately, hit the sweet spots of their hardcore fanbase. Hence, in 2003, an anime and two video games were born (for starters). *The Animatrix,* written but not directed by the Wachowskis, composed of nine animated shorts, expanding the fictional universe of *The Matrix.* The anime provided enough story fodder to build up to the release of the original's sequel, *The Matrix Reloaded,* also in 2003. That year continued to be very busy with the release of two video games, *Matrix: Path of Neo* and *Enter the Matrix,* which explained some mysteries of the previous films and cleared up any head scratching over continuity* in preparation for the final film of the trilogy,

---

* For example, the change in appearance of the Oracle character. In the game's fiction, it was explained as a result of an attack by Merovingian. In reality, actress Gloria Foster had passed away and was replaced by Mary Alice.

The Matrix Revolutions (quick note: the Wachowskis wrote and directed both the films and those games). Two years later, in 2005, a massively multiplayer online game (MMO) came out entitled *The Matrix Online*, which contained enough backstory for the final film, *The Matrix Revolutions*, to retroactively* qualify as its prequel. From 1999 to 2004, the franchise also had a series of webcomics that provided ancillary narrative to give fans additional adventures of characters they loved. But the comics did not have a direct connection to the films, anime, or games. (The exception being "Bits and Pieces of Information" written by the Wachowskis, but that was adapted into the short film "The Second Renaissance" as part of *The Animatrix*.)† While the quality of the films tended to dwindle one after the other, *The Matrix* franchise validated the power of transmedia by showing that an IP is not defined by one medium. Its DNA dictates what other forms it should take (Figure 5).

Why Are Video Games a Natural Fit for Transmedia?

Most games, as with most media, are not designed with a transmedia component. Some might argue that the marketing campaign for a game qualifies as one. However, the occasional tweet or Instagram post that promotes the game in the voice of the company isn't even close to a transmedia campaign. Overt marketing is just an obvious series of branded media overtures to persuade fans to buy a product. But if the campaign was executed through the voices of the game's characters? And in different media? With permanent impact on the lore? That's a different story. That's actual storytelling. And depending on how immersive the campaign is (that is, how long the characters are conveying the fiction), the storytelling could even be good.

Successful game franchises over the past decade have leveraged transmedia to great success. Titles like *Assassin's Creed, Halo, Mass Effect, Batman: Arkham Asylum*, and their respective sequels have generated impressive sales figures. One can attribute their success not only to the quality of their games, but also to the transmedia efforts of their studios. Each made sure to publish books and comics and produce animation or digital content to build up to the release of a game. Yes, these satisfied a marketing purpose; however, these transmedia extensions also expanded

---

* The MMO came out in 2005, but in the story chronology of the franchise, it actually takes places before *The Matrix Revolutions*, which came out in 2003.
† (Jenkins 2006: 120)

FIGURE 5 Story Chronology of *The Matrix* Franchise.

the universe of these games and even became memorable products in their own right. In November 2007, *Halo: Contact Harvest* by Joseph Staten debuted on The New York Times Best Seller list at #3.* This book was not an adaptation of one of the games. It was a separate narrative that took place 27 years before the 2001 hit *Halo: Combat Evolved.*

While the book came out two months after *Halo 3* – that year's anchor property for the franchise – the book's November release helped increase game sales leading into the Christmas season. By early January of 2008, the game sold over 8.1 million copies.† As of this writing, *Halo 3* has sold over 14.5 million copies.‡

The video game industry is a testament to the fact that transmedia is a risk worth taking. But how the industry got to embrace transmedia is a result of the culture of the industry and its fans.

Competitive Edge

Games are a hyper-competitive business. Companies are always looking for the newest advantage over their rivals. The industry is also one that welcomes innovation, from graphics to audio to gameplay. Story is also part of that innovation, but not in the traditional sense.

Story in games is less about the conventional way stories are told (as described previously), but more about its fictional universe and characters. What is it about this world that draws me in and makes me want to live in it? What is it about the weapons of the characters that I want to use for myself? What is it about the villain's mysterious presence that I want to learn more about? Not all games engender this type of curiosity. But a select few make sure to answer those questions not just in the games, but in the transmedia.

However, transmedia-friendly franchises like *Halo, Assassin's Creed,* and *Mass Effect* don't typically tie their transmedia into a single-story experience. The transmedia extensions are usually opportunities to explore deeper into a franchise's universe. You'll find origins of world events or revelations of character backgrounds. But we have yet to see a protagonist's journey that is told continuously from one of these media to the next.

---

* (Cavalli 2007)
† ("Halo" n.d.)
‡ ("Halo 3" n.d.)

Game developers don't want to lose customers by immersing them in a game story that won't make sense unless they read the book or watch the animated series that came beforehand. The safest bet instead is to create an unrelated story to the game narrative. This story is still important because it provides context to the world and answers small mysteries about the game universe (e.g., *Halo*'s John-117 reveal).

Is it too much to ask of consumers to experience all of the franchise's media in a certain sequence in order to appreciate it fully? Maybe. But it's an important challenge to solve in the future, as the new generation of media consumers are so tied to their tech and are consummate multi-taskers. One day, it will not be outrageous for them to watch a full season of a Netflix show and visit social media channels to experience the fictional characters' online activities as a meaningful tie-in to the next season of that Netflix show. And when the next season picks up, it's likely that there will be enough drama in there that is independent of what happened on social media so that new followers won't feel left out. But you can bet the farm that a substantial amount of that show's minor storylines will have significant references to the social media drama.

Traditional console games might ultimately stick with the self-contained transmedia off-shoots that they do now. But with the promise of Virtual Reality and Augmented Reality – and Mixed Reality! – a seamless and enduring transmedia experience might not be far off. But first, one has to prove the promise of AR actually delivers. And *Pokémon GO* has done just that.

How it works: players use their smartphones to locate Pokémon in places (aka PokeStops or PokeGyms) in their natural environment but are translated in the visual language of the virtual Pokémon world on the screen of a smartphone. This requires players to go outside and interact with parts of their natural environment, near or far. To top it off, they can physically work side-by-side, in real time, with other players to catch these Pokémon together (either through a "king of the hill" mechanic or – if a gamer is working alone – through flicking a ball at it). Not much of a narrative experience, but revolutionary nonetheless. The developer of this one-time blockbuster AR experience, Niantic Labs, chartered this territory a few years earlier with *Ingress*, a massively multiplayer online real-time strategy (MMORTS) mobile game, which had a rich lore, but no identifiable protagonist. To play, gamers must choose a side – either the Resistance or the Enlightened – and collaborate with others on the same side to obtain alien fragments known as Exotic Matter. The Resistance wants to prevent it from getting it in the hands of the Enlightened, who want to use it as a way to enhance or transcend human beings. However, the Resistance believes that, due to the alien nature of Exotic Matter, any integration with human biology could spell the end of the human race. Players track and collect these digital fragments of Exotic Matter through their phones, a practice known as geocaching (which *Pokémon GO* thrived on as well). Collection locales correspond to real-world locations, but are repurposed through their phone as part of the *Ingress* sci-fi environment.

In addition to its AR capabilities, *Ingress* was also a successful trans-media experience focused on the constant friction between the Resistance and the Enlightened through live-action videos and live event gaming. Story installments were delivered through videos, akin to news pieces that depicted the progress of each side at a high level. The lore was inde-pendent of the actions you – the player – made. But by working with thousands of others across the world, players could influence the nar-rative. Subsequent videos would acknowledge (usually on a daily basis) which side was winning in the hunt for Exotic Matter and in the struggle to defend or transcend humankind. However, moving the needle in the ongoing battle between the Resistance and the Enlightened would be a group effort with no call-outs to individual players. The daily video responses were, accordingly, generic to player action, but specific to the lore of the world.

The joy of *Ingress* hinges upon collaboration with strangers across the world. Based on the time of day that you play, you could always find a group of players in your faction who are also on the hunt for Exotic Matter. They'll be collecting in real-world places and will rely on you to do the same. The rarer the Exotic Matter, the more sense of accomplishment you and your fellow players will have. This type of cooperative play was unprecedented in the mobile space at the time of its launch in 2012. *Ingress* is a revolutionary experience not only because of that, but also because it paved the way for AR to become a customer-facing reality.

The more the technology expands, the more the players will demand that their stories mold to these technologies. *Ingress* and *Pokémon GO* brought players into experiences that were simultaneously real world and augmented. But why stop there? If players are interested in a continuous ongoing search, how far away are we from adding social media into the mix to help players, for example, find other Pokémon? Could there be a Twitter "mole" that gives cryptic clues to the fans, informing them of the vague proximity and time of when to find a rare Pokémon?

Could there be a virtual marketplace where you could trade Pokémon, even getting backstory for each character through an animated series? For rare Pokémon, is their story told through a comic that increases their value and desirability?

Even if the appetite for this kind of social media integration isn't there yet, Augmented Reality is fertile ground for innovative transmedia storytelling. One more blockbuster experience is all that it takes to help AR reach critical mass.

Early Adopters

Most people who consume transmedia are often early adopters of new technology. They view anything that is innovative in the realm of story – for example, how the content is delivered and the technology that delivers it – as a necessary experience to consume. Transmedia fans are story zealots. They have an insatiable appetite for the omnipresence of story. A fictional character's tweets will gain just as much devotion as a new episode of an animated series from that character's fictional universe.

And games, perhaps due to their addictive nature, have always attracted a more intense, zealous consumer. Not all gamers are story zealots (or even fans of story). But those who are will likely consume everything about the brand of that game – shirts, toys, books, comics, movies, TV shows, podcasts, social media channels, and more.

A video game is also that rare entity that is both a vehicle for story and, in itself, technology (read: software). Games can also be media extensions of beloved brands that came from another medium like film (such as *Star Wars*; Marvel Universe; DC Universe). But games are more often the original medium from which other media extensions emerge (for example, *Halo, Mass Effect, Assassins Creed,* and *Skylanders*). The *Halo* franchise has spawned numerous books, even one – as mentioned earlier – that made it to The New York Times Best Seller list. It has also spawned a successful toy franchise with Mega Bloks. In 2012, the Emmy-nominated *Forward unto Dawn* captured the attention of millions as a digital mini-series on YouTube and Waypoint (*Halo's* proprietary information site). It served as live-action lead-in to the much-anticipated *Halo 4*, one of the first games available exclusively for the Xbox One. And most recently, a series drama is being developed by Showtime. In between game releases, fans of the franchise have had plenty of transmedia material to satisfy their *Halo* appetite. While most of that material is not tied together in any sequential order (in fact, some of the books are centered on past wars that are only referenced in the games), one could argue that *Halo* set the standard for transmedia storytelling for the games industry. More on this later.

Greatest Transmedia Campaign Ever?

During a job interview, a game producer asked me what I thought was the best transmedia experience in the last five years. This was in 2011, so I quickly rummaged through my memory and recalled all the huge successes in transmedia since 2006 – *Halo 3* and the *I Love Bees* alternative reality game ("ARG"); *The Dark Knight* and *Why So Serious?* ARG; *lonelyGirl15*; *Prom Queen* ... Then it hit me.

In late 2007, Barack Obama eclipsed Hillary Clinton as the Democratic favorite for the 2008 Presidential election. Every story about him – be it in commercials, news pieces, interviews – painted a very compelling portrait of a junior senator from Illinois who wasn't well known until then. While the conventional media swooned over him, social media showed that Obama wasn't just a news item; he was a personal hero to voiceless millions who were excited about a genuine change candidate. Through sharing news pieces about him and engaging in conversation with friends over Facebook, voters cemented their loyalty. They would serve as devoted soldiers in his army of "clicktivists." Without having any connection to his campaign, fans would do their part to get people excited about his candidacy. They did it out of pure enthusiasm for a man who rekindled people's faith in the democratic process.

Fans would soon create their own videos – without much production value, mind you – that complemented those that the Obama campaign created themselves. The online discussions and videos were owned by a younger demographic, particularly young Gen-Xers and Millennials.

By the time the results of the Iowa caucuses came in, Barack Obama had quickly emerged as the clear frontrunner. Losses in New Hampshire, South Carolina, and many Super Tuesday states had tightened the race once again in Hillary Clinton's favor. But by February 12th, after winning District of Columbia, Maryland, and Virginia, it was clear that Obama's momentum was not going to end. His path to becoming the first African American candidate for President of a major political party was sealed.

Thereafter, Obama's presence was everywhere – social media, TV ads, live events (rallies, interviews, debates), even in video games (as ads that appear before a menu screen). His story was clear: Change. No matter what outlet he was on, people knew that voting for Barack Obama was about voting for a completely new look, new way, and new attitude of what it means to be president … and to be an American. Americans were in the midst of a terrible economy, created by the old guard. Nearly seven years of unpopular wars decimated our morale. This was brought on, once again, by the old guard. Barack Obama was a superhero, who would free us from the grips of selfish politicians, war mongers, and corrupt bankers.

His campaign was transmedia storytelling at its finest. His story was clear in every media touchpoint: we knew who the characters were (protagonist: Barack Obama; antagonist: the Establishment *ala* Hillary Clinton, George W. Bush, and John McCain), and we saw the rise of his heroism amidst escalating burdens (the 3 am White House Telephone Call ad; the Muslim extremist accusations; the collapse of Lehman Brothers).

2008 was an exciting time to be a voter, to be an American. It was also an exciting time to witness one of the greatest stories about a politician to unfold before our eyes. My telling this is neither an endorsement nor a rejection of Barack Obama. It is, instead, a depiction of how transmedia storytelling can be a powerful force in our lives.

THE BASICS

What can we learn from the Barack Obama campaign as it applies to transmedia storytelling? While not all IP or brands are the same, there are several immutable guidelines to adopt when telling your story across different media platforms.

Identify the main medium of the anchor property. What is the main medium through which the hero's story is told? Is it a film that will have sequels? If so, then the transmedia extensions will serve as their connective tissue. Similar thinking must be applied to a TV show. Will digital videos tie one season to the next during a hiatus (like in *The Office: The Accountants* in 2007)? Or will it be web comics to galvanize excitement from episode to episode, as we saw with the TV series *Heroes*? Or is the focus on a figure, like a presidential candidate? In this case, the anchor property is where that figure will get the most attention, and usually that is through television. Each major appearance (like a debate or a nomination acceptance speech) will be the climactic moments to which all the transmedia extensions build up.

Make the hero clear and upfront. Let your audience know whom the story is about at any given moment and why we should care about him/her. Without this, you have nothing.

Your story must migrate from at least two different media platforms in a meaningful way. Telling your story from one television series to another is not an example of transmedia. That is a strict example of a crossover. It's a very popular strategy in television, in particular, as it drives audiences from one show to the other in the hope that both shows retain new viewers after the crossover storyline is complete. *The Practice* and *Ally McBeal* did this in the late '90s, as did *Magnum PI* and *Simon & Simon* in the '80s. It's more common today within the Marvel Universe. Before the Netflix relationship with Disney came to a close in 2019, beloved Marvel characters like Daredevil, Jessica Jones, Iron Fist, and Luke Cage made appearances in the others' shows as a lead up to *The Defenders* Netflix TV series. In the DC universe, Flash and Green Arrow have been crossing over into each other's shows on the CW since the 2014/2015 season.

But transmedia storytelling requires more. In fact, the name itself implies traveling across ("trans") different media. *Quantum Break* (video game/TV mini-series) and *Batman: Arkham Asylum* (game franchise/comic series) are popular examples of a story continuing from one medium to the next while tying back to the initial medium (in this case, games).

Be consistent with the sentiment across all platforms. If you're dividing a story into four parts and assigning each part to a new medium, make sure the spirit of the story remains the same. Viewers or players might consume these parts out of order, so you want them to feel something about the hero's story that's consistently told. You want to reinforce the positivity they have about the hero and the world.

Discoverability is everything! If the consumer is only familiar with one medium of a campaign (for example: digital videos), make sure there is information somewhere within that medium (either as an end credit or as part of the description underneath the video itself) to drive people to the other media. And make this process as easy to find as possible, even if it compromises some of the immersion.

Know your endpoint and make sure everything leads to it. Knowing how and when your campaign ends will dictate: (1) when certain media is released; (2) what the media type is, per release; and (3) what part of the story will be released. This requires a very specific plotting of each release and can resemble the story milestones described in Chapter #6 – "Structure" – of this book. If, however, you're not putting out a single story, but multiple stories, then you must keep the endpoint in mind and view every media release before the tent-pole premiere *as its own medium*. It's important to map out the 30,000-foot view of the experience from beginning to end. A structure diagram similar to what I provided in Chapter #10 will be a good starting point. Then ask yourself: Under what act of the experience does the media extension fall? Does it continue where the previous medium left off? If so, assign structural milestones inside each extension. Or is each extension completely new and separate from one another? Then know the grammar for that medium and craft a self-contained structure for it. Refer to Chapter #6 to adapt your story beats accordingly.

Encourage fan participation. You know your IP has made it when fans start creating their own media related to it. This shows organic brand activism. IP stakeholders will want to encourage this more because a dedicated fanbase, even if small, will consume your IP in large doses and endlessly advocate for it. These brand activists could be social media influencers, who discuss your product over YouTube, Twitch, Twitter, and Instagram and consequently promote your brand to their vast following. Another incarnation of a brand activist is a fan fiction author, who writes alternative plotlines to an established book often without the author's permission. While changing the names of the characters and adding slight alterations to the plot can lead to a massive success without fear of a lawsuit,* most fan fiction has no intention of getting published or catapulting a fledgling author to stardom. Its goal is to pay homage to an IP that has brought tremendous joy to a devoted following and to encourage them to let their imagination run wild with the characters they love so much. What this generates is long-term excitement for a brand or IP; therefore, when its next installment is launched, devoted fans will be chomping at the bit to buy/see/play/read it and tell their friends about it, thereby increasing the consumer base. Movies, games, and books are no longer self-contained media experiences. At bare minimum, the creators will be reaching out to fans through social media. Fans will, in turn, continue the conversation *ad infinitum* with other fans. If they feel slighted in any way, this will affect sales, ratings, viewership, or any other form of consumer goodwill. With so much competition out there, a brand or IP cannot afford to omit fans at any point of its promotion.

Know the grammar of each medium through which your story is migrating. Writing for television is not the same as writing for games. Writing for games is not the same as writing for comics. Writing for comics is not the same as writing for a live event. Writing for a live event is not the same as writing for a podcast. You get the picture. Each medium requires

---

* *Fifty Shades of Grey,* for instance, was originally an R-rated fan fiction exploration of the *Twilight* characters.

a different rule-set, including: length; where to focus one's attention; what the modality is (visual, audio, etc.); and more. When your story crosses numerous media pathways, fans will not appreciate a "shoe-horned" story experience in a comic if they know it's a better fit for a film. The IP will be judged not just as a holistic experience, but also for its disparate parts.

THE PURPOSE

It's very easy for storytellers to "geek out" on how their story is told. (Often, this zealous focus can take away from the quality of the story itself, so beware.) Without knowing your audience, however, one runs the risk of creating a transmedia experience just for the sake of it. That's a waste of time and money; even more so, a vacant transmedia experience diminishes the story and burns consumer goodwill. The TV show *Defiance* (2013–2015) is a perfect example of this. This obscure TV show on the Syfy Network thought it could push the boundaries of storytelling by offering a supplemental, but thinly related MMO. Neither the TV show nor the game was any good, and abysmal ratings and miniscule daily active users of the game killed the franchise.

Therefore, it's crucial to identify the business case for the transmedia campaign before you pursue it. Consider:

- *Brand reinforcement and brand omnipresence.* Once you identify the anchor property of the experience, use the transmedia connective tissue not only to continue the story of the anchor property, but also to create awareness of it. Have a presence on all social media platforms to reinforce the brand, but refrain from typical marketing. *"Superhero X comes to theaters on March 23rd"* is exactly what to avoid. Instead, use the voices of the characters from *Superhero X* to engage the audience. Include the requisite hashtags and @s to drive viewers to the typical marketing accounts, but always remember you are telling a story, so it's crucial to sustain the immersion.

- *Expansion of the fiction.* Before the launch of every *Assassin's Creed* video game sequel, game publisher Ubisoft partnered up with comic publishers, traditional publishers, and animation production teams to expand the fiction in their respective medium as a way to spur excitement for the game. It worked both ways, of course: a popular video game franchise would also spark sales for the other media. Through licensing, the books and comics also offered a secondary income stream for Ubisoft. But the primary goal of these transmedia extensions was to create awareness for new customers of the game. If, for instance, you stumble upon the book or comic and like what you read, perhaps you'll buy the game.

- *Consumer goodwill.* Transmedia experiences are effective because they appeal to a consumer's convenience. Thanks to social media and mobile technologies, one can visit the social media accounts of an IP at their leisure; same too with reading a web comic or watching a digital short on his/her phone. These disruptive technologies have upended the traditional "water cooler moment," where people would convene in the office to discuss what happened in last night's episode of a favorite show or an opening of a highly anticipated movie. With the exception of a popular sports event (like the Super Bowl or the final game of the NBA Finals), there is little in the media marketplace today that is universally watched at the same time, thus preventing the gathering of people to talk about it. Audiences today are fractured. Today's surfeit of media has made consumers highly selective, hyper-specialized, and incredibly demanding. When they devote their time to a movie, game, show, or book, they're all in. They will binge-watch a series in an entire weekend, read all the social media responses about it, and consume all of the other supporting media. With that level of commitment from consumers, content creators cannot – under any circumstances – under-serve their fanbase. There's a ton of competition out there, so the fans can go elsewhere quickly. Also, the fans' level of enthusiasm of an IP corresponds to the IP's longevity. Fan intensity and positivity have a strong financial impact on an IP. They will buy all the merchandise related to it. Capturing and sustaining their enthusiasm are not only about profit, however. The more valuable currency is conversation. The more the fans discuss an IP on social media (or even traditional media), the more others become aware of it and consume it. If the fanbase senses they are being disrespected, conversation will not only sour; it will eventually halt. By then, the IP is dead in the water.

- *KPIs.* Lastly, you'll need to determine what will make the transmedia experience a success. Key performance indicators (KPIs) such as increased followers on social media, sales figures for transmedia extensions (like e-books or ad revenue for a YouTube series), and merchandising sales are good markers of the effectiveness of the transmedia. More importantly, did the anchor property get considerably more ratings/box office receipts/sales as a result of the campaign? Determining specific numbers for each KPI will help drive the budget and make sound creative decisions. Regarding the latter, creative decisions can be altered in the middle of a campaign if certain characters or plot points in the transmedia extensions are not being well received. Granted, the changes cannot be wholesale and will be moderate at best. For instance, if a character from a graphic novel is not trending well two months before the premiere of a film, it's impossible to change that character in that upcoming film. However, the social media accounts for these characters can change instantly or at least address what's not tracking well. Last-minute viral videos can mollify discontent. At the very least, the data from these consumer reactions can effectuate meaningful changes in the next installment of the transmedia campaign. Fans might have to wait a while, especially if the anchor property is a film or video game. Sequels take time to develop.

TWO KINDS OF TRANSMEDIA EXPERIENCES

When crafting your campaign, it's important to determine how immersive you want the experience to be. Do you want fans to have 100% engagement through the characters of the fiction? Is there a breaking-the-fourth-wall moment where characters will talk to fans to inform them of, say, a launch of a related app? Or will that marketing ploy kill the fiction? Above all, you must identify how patient and enthusiastic your fanbase is. Are they dedicated enough to follow every coordinate of your story's migration? Are they tech-savvy enough to engage in interactive moments? Are they extroverted enough to participate in a live event? A proper gauge of your fans' appetite will dictate what kind of transmedia experience you'll want to create.

A Pure, Singular Story Experience

As mentioned earlier in this chapter, a pure transmedia experience aims to tell one unified story across different media. Imagine if the first season of Disney's *Daredevil* was repurposed accordingly: Matt Murdock's initial rise as Daredevil and threat to archnemesis Wilson Fisk happen in five episodes of a Netflix series. Then, you continue his path toward taking down Fisk in a video game. But before Fisk is arrested (like in the first season of the show), you reserve that final confrontation in a graphic novel.

Realistically, most fans will not join you as you go from one medium to the next. Pure transmedia experiences are for the true fans; they will ride with you until the car runs out of gas. But for everyone else (that is, the majority), you cannot design the story experience to have its biggest moments in its smallest media. That's just not good business savvy. Whether it's the death of a sidekick or the destruction of a home planet, certain moments are so profound that they must be delivered through the medium that attracts the most eye balls and the biggest dollars. That medium is usually a film, video game, or TV series. Comics, novels, digital series, amusement park rides, and other extensions have a supplemental purpose in transmedia: to explain past story beats, focus on beloved supporting characters, reveal mysteries of the lore, and carry forward minor plot points introduced in the anchor property.

I classify these transmedia off-shoots as "in the wild" because they can easily live independently of the anchor property, even if they push forward minor plot points. A creator may never know if a player or consumer found their way to the tent-pole product through the transmedia extension. Nor can the creator control how a player or consumer will experience the story. Do they play the game first and then check out the comic series? Do they read the comic series first, put it down, and pick up the game months later and forget the connection between the two? Again, there's no controlling the behaviors of fans. And that should not be a priority for creators. Examples of pure, singular story experiences with "in the wild" transmedia include: *The Matrix* franchise (three films, three video games, and an anime are directly connected in telling a unified story); the game *Batman: Arkham Asylum* and the comic *The Road to Arkham*; *Forward Unto Dawn* digital series and *Halo 4* video game; *Til Morning's Light* video game and its audiobook *Til Morning's Light: The Private Blog of Erica Page*; *lonelygirl15* digital series and its alternative reality games (ARGs).*

To guarantee that fans will travel from the original medium to another, you may want to design for a closed ecosystem – as in, a multi-media or multi-modal experience within one product that is interacted upon the moment you buy it (or stream it or download it). *Quantum Break*, for example, is an experience that is part video game, part TV series. You could not watch the series on television at a specific time of day. It was sealed on the disc on the game, and episodes would unlock after a player

---

* Upon full disclosure, I was a writer for the latter two IPs as well as the narrative designer for the previously mentioned *Quantum Break*.

successfully accomplished objectives. Everything was "on rails," which meant a player couldn't unlock an episode without playing through a specific proscribed path. The YA novel *Cathy's Book: If Found Call (650) 266-8233* by Sean Stewart and Jordan Weisman was designed as a closed ecosystem as well. Readers could take part in an ARG just by following clues from the pages of the book.

Fractured Experience about the World

The other type of transmedia experience takes into account that most fans will not have the bandwidth or interest to follow the evolution of a single-story experience across various media. However, because they like the characters of the world so much, fans will consume whatever they can just as long as it doesn't require too much time or devotion. This is the most popular form of transmedia storytelling. Creators cannot expect the consumer to buy every comic, watch every digital series, or play every level of a single game to a franchise they've paid good money for. The average consumer does not want the pressure to follow everything. Expecting too much of them is inviting disaster. People consume entertainment to escape, not to do homework.

Under this framework, this transmedia experience doesn't tell a single story that ties all the disparate media together. This framework relies, instead, on lighter connective tissue between the tent-pole* releases. Supporting characters, commonly travelled worlds, and shared fictional events that are referred to from tent-pole to tent-pole are sufficient connective tissue. Fans won't feel like they are missing out if they didn't play the last installment of the *Defiance* MMO even though they watched every episode of the show. Or an introduction of a new character (Hana Gitelman) in a *Heroes* episode will be exciting for fans of the TV series, but might seem redundant to those who read the web comic religiously. The stories in the MMO and web comic take on a life of their own, but must be designed thoughtfully in order to feel related to their anchor properties.

The Clone Wars animated series has done a fairly good job at expanding the *Star Wars* prequel mythology in between *Episode II: Attack of*

---

* As a refresher, tent-pole properties are the big event productions from a single company. There could be multiple tent-pole properties in one year – as is the case with the Marvel Cinematic Universe – or in successive years, as is the case with the *Star Wars* sequel trilogy films. With those franchises being the exceptions, tent-poles aren't typically related to one another. Their monstrous budgets, however, classify them as such. For further reference, check out Anita Elberse's *Blockbusters: Hit-Making, Risk-taking, and the Big Business of Entertainment* (2013).

the Clone Wars and *Episode III: Revenge of the Sith*. One doesn't have to watch the animated series to understand what's going on in the sequels. However, *The Clone Wars* is an excellent source of expanding the fictional universe of *Star Wars* and providing retroactive "aha" moments when lore references are made in the films.

And, of course, there are experiences that can be too fractured. Take, for instance, *The X-Files*. At the height of its popularity in the late 1990s, *The X-Files* TV series did something that no series did beforehand: it had a mainstream release of a blockbuster film – *The X-Files: Fight the Future*. In fact, it generated over $189 million in worldwide box office revenue.* Despite its success, the movie was written as a self-contained story so that newcomers to the franchise didn't need to watch the series to understand what's going on. However, loyal fans of the show found the writing to be disjointed and inelegant. The momentum of the conflicts with old enemies, such as the Cigarette Smoking Man, was undercut and derailed in an effort to focus on new villains in the film. By the time the next season started, there was no reference to any of the new characters from the film. It was as if it never existed. The film was basically a two-hour episode with the occasional swear word.

The X-Files film was an isolated moment in the lore of the show, and ultimately a cheap exploitation of fan loyalty. For something as big as a feature film seen by a fanbase as vast as any TV show up to that moment, the show creators were obliged to move the franchise forward. This means that whatever happened in the film must have, at least, a minor downstream effect on the next season of the series, such as expansion of the lore or new juicy secrets about characters we've been invested in for 5 years. That was not the case. Sadly, this was a missed opportunity as was the next film *The X-Files: I Want to Believe* ten years later.

Sacrificial Lambs

There will be some media that won't get high ratings or purchases. That's not their goal. They exist solely to bridge the gaps between one big-budget medium to the next. The American version of the TV series *The Office* produced a digital series entitled *The Accountants*, which premiered the summer before the third season. The ten episodes of the digital series aired on the NBC website on Thursday, and were no more than 3 minutes apiece. The series won a Creative Emmy for "Outstanding Broadband

---

* ("The X-Files" 1998)

Program – Comedy" in 2007.* The producers of the show continued to produce a new digital series for every season afterwards. In 2008, the digital series was split into two installments: once in the summer, once during a mid-season hiatus. In 2009–2011, the two installments varied in release dates. Each installment was a different story arc and continued to focus on the supporting characters of the show.

The purpose, from a narrative perspective, was to provide deeper explorations of characters that didn't have much screen time in the regular series. From a business standpoint, the digital series was a device that galvanized fanbase loyalty and excitement. It didn't matter if the content was short; it just mattered to feed the fans so that they could continue watching the show. That, in many ways, is the bulk of the work of transmedia: to provide continual content in between seasons or tent-pole sequels. "Feed the beast," as I call it. Fans want to be nourished and tended to. Without a high-budget film running a perpetual story 24/7, the next best thing is "bread-crumbing" content to fans through transmedia continually.

MEDIA RELEASE STRATEGIES

A compelling transmedia campaign will design everything around the anchor property. The lead-in to its release is the most important part of the entire campaign. Books, a digital series, or a comic series excites the fanbase and "prime the pump" for the anchor property's release.

In film, the producers of *Prometheus* launched a series of digital shorts on YouTube, months before the film's opening. Each served as a backstory fragment of the life of the film's antagonist, Peter Weyland. The number of hits was modest, but the box office for the film surpassed $400 million. It's possible that the digital shorts, which featured actors from the movie, suffered from issues of discoverability, not of quality.

Games have done a much better job at prepping the release of tent-pole products. *Halo, Mass Effect,* and *Assassin's Creed,* once again, are known for extending the universe of their games through books, comics, board games, animated features, and web series. They also know how to continue the momentum of fan enthusiasm by filling in the gaps in between tent-pole releases with smaller games. These games don't continue the main narrative, but they are canonical by focusing on a different part of the game's lore. To address these gaps, the transmedia release schedule is very

---

* ("34th Annual Creative Arts & Entertainment Emmy Awards Presented at Star-Studded Hollywood Gala" 2007)

critical. How to carry the interest of fans is part art, part science. When are fans more likely to buy your IP's books and comics? This is a question answered through competitive analysis. When are your rivals putting out their next game? When is the market least saturated? Which months does your prime demographic spend the most money? These are the science questions.

The main art question is, "How do you prevent overexposure of your IP?" Fans are fickle. When they've had enough, they'll let you know by not consuming your product. By then, it'll be too late because there will be no other chances to regain their interest. That's why it's important to involve user researchers early on to test the "stickiness" of your IP and use their data to pivot strategies. A robust transmedia campaign is ideal, but if your team is not in sync with your fanbase's level of oversaturation, it doesn't matter how great your content is. Your IP is done.

Smart transmedia campaigns cluster content around the release of the anchor property. There's usually a book or comic series release a week to a month before the game comes out. Additional media will come out a day to a month afterwards. A good example is a weekly digital series, like *Halo: Nightfall* (see Figure 6). The weekly episodes should provide enough momentum for the IP to endure well after its release date. Reviewers and fans will take it from there. There might be more related media that comes out toward the end of the year as a way to generate interest for Christmas.

If the IP is an ongoing franchise with a big tent-pole product release every three years (as many big games have), then studios can fill in the gap years with the releases of lesser-budgeted games for console, mobile, or PC. Lower hanging fruit is the key here. As such, books and comics will come to market as well, not only to support these smaller game releases, but also to pique the interest of the fanbase and retain their loyalty until the next tent-pole product release. The following graph is a transmedia timeline for the *Halo* franchise, one of the biggest tent-pole franchises in Microsoft's entire games portfolio (as well as one of the biggest game franchises ever). Its two decades as a successful video game franchise are not only a testament to its being a great game; its sustained transmedia storytelling through books, comics, and digital series has been a crucial factor as well. The graph starts from the initial release of *Halo* and ends at the release of *Halo 5*. Due to the vast output of the franchise, not all of the transmedia extensions are represented here (Figure 6).

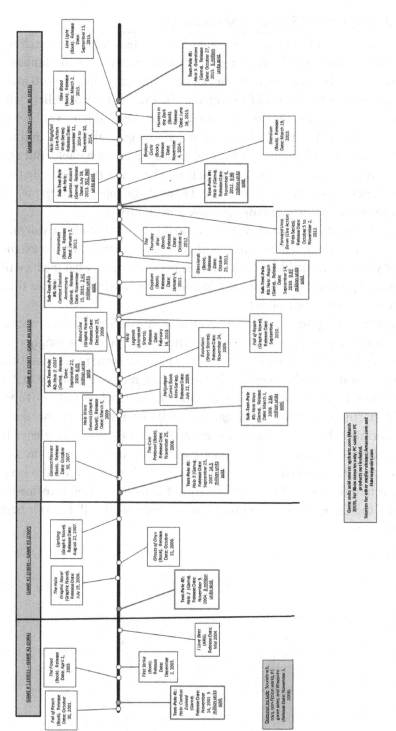

FIGURE 6 Halo Transmedia Timeline. (See full-scale version of this graph at www.crcpress.com/9781138319738.)

FINAL THOUGHTS ON TRANSMEDIA

How stories are told will continue to advance with technology. Storytelling will also evolve with the media consumption patterns of the fanbase. Media that can be accessed any time but on a constant drip feed – no matter the length or the source of that media – is the future. Storytellers will need to learn how to shape the content output and harness it to avoid, what I call, IP fatigue. Yes, there can be too much of a good thing. Dwindling sales/gross receipts/ratings of a beloved franchise are inevitable. But the opportunity is extending the life of the franchise at the right pace. Be like *Seinfeld*: never overstay your welcome. Leave at the top of your game, so that consumer goodwill remains positive and enduring.

Not all franchises need to have transmedia. That's something you and your team will need to determine. Will your players appreciate the extension of your world outside of the gaming experience? If so, what media will the players gravitate to? How much do you want to feed them so that they are excited to play your game?

Another thing to consider: transmedia storytelling isn't a necessary component of the narrative of a game. However, it is strongly recommended to adopt if one's goal is to create an enduring franchise that feeds its customers wherever they're consuming media. It is likely that a gamer is on social media and digital platforms like Twitch and YouTube, either sharing their love of the game or following someone who does. Transforming that from a spectator experience into a story experience is a delicate one. Success depends heavily on how you want to use the fiction of your game to penetrate these sacred areas. You might want to keep the spectator element completely free from the fiction. If not, transmedia storytelling through the "Fractured World" framework will be your best option.

CHAPTER 14

Addendum

LIST OF UNIVERSITIES FOR GAME DEVELOPMENT

If you're looking to pursue a degree in game development, there is a growing list of colleges and universities to choose from. In fact, you'll find some of the most prestigious institutions in engineering on that list. They understand that video games aren't some flimsy diversion; they require as much programming and design savvy as traditional software does ... maybe even more so. They've developed robust design and engineering programs to train the next generation of innovators in entertainment and interactive technology.

The following list is not comprehensive by any means, but it should give you a broad view of the types of institutions out there, be they for-profit or non-profit, public or private.* These schools provide at least one course in game narrative, but there is no guarantee of its frequency. University of Southern California, Rensselaer Institute of Technology, and MIT have been pretty consistent in their offerings of narrative coursework. Contact the following universities directly and see what courses they have on narrative design and game writing.

I've included the following institutions in particular because I have worked directly with many of their alumni and can vouch for their high level of preparedness. But, again, there are plenty of alumni from other great schools doing great work. I recommend checking out www.gamedesigning.org for more information.

---

* Please note: the spelling of the degrees is varied and customized to the preference of the university (for example, Master of Science vs. Master's of Science).

Not-for-profit, Private Colleges/Universities

- **Carnegie Mellon University**

  Entertainment Technology Center

  Pittsburgh, PA

  www.etc.cmu.edu

  Offers: Master of Entertainment Technology*

- **Massachusetts Institute of Technology**

  Comparative Media Studies/Writing Program

  Cambridge, MA

  https://cmsw.mit.edu/

  Offers: Scientiae Baccalaureus (Bachelor of Science) in Comparative Media Studies; Scientiae Baccalaureus (Bachelor of Science) in Digital Media; and Scientiae Magister (Master of Science) in Comparative Media Studies

- **New York University**

  Interactive Telecommunications Program (part of Tisch School of the Arts)

  New York, NY

  https://tisch.nyu.edu/itp

  Offers: Master of Professional Studies[†]

- **Rensselaer Institute of Technology**

  Games and Simulation and Arts and Sciences

  Troy, NY

  http://www.hass.rpi.edu/pl/gaming

  Offers: Bachelor of Science in Games and Simulation Arts and Sciences[‡]

---

[*] Undergraduate students can seek a Minor in Game Design through the university's Integrative Design, Arts, and Technology program. Visit www.ideate.cmu.edu for more details.

[†] NYU also offers a Bachelor of Fine Arts in Interactive Media Arts.

[‡] The university also offers a Bachelor of Science and a PhD in a related field known as Electronic Arts. A Master of Fine Arts program is currently being revamped.

- **University of Southern California**

  Interactive Media & Games Division (part of the School of Cinematic Arts)

  Los Angeles, CA

  cinema.usc.edu/interactive/index.cfm

  Offers: Bachelors of Arts in Interactive Entertainment* ; Master of Fine Arts in Interactive Media; Master of Arts in Cinematic Arts (Media Arts, Games and Health)

Not-for-profit, Public Colleges/Universities

- **Michigan State University**

  Game Design and Development Program Dev Program

  East Lansing, MI

  gamedev.msu.edu

  Offers: Bachelors of Arts in Media and Information; Masters of Arts in Media and Information; PhD in Information and Media

- **University of California, Irvine**

  Donald Bren School of Information & Computer Sciences

  Irvine, CA

  https://www.ics.uci.edu/about/

  Offers: Bachelor of Science in Computer Game Science†

- **University of California, Santa Cruz**

  Santa Cruz, CA

  https://admissions.sa.ucsc.edu/majors/artgamemedia

  Offers: Bachelor of Arts in Art & Design: Games & Playable Media

---

* Made possible through the Dornsife College of Letters, Arts, and Sciences. The undergraduate major is in conjunction with the School of Cinematic Arts.

† UCI is home to a deep gaming culture. In addition to its forward-thinking undergraduate studies, it is also the first public university to offer an eSports program.

- **University of Central Florida**

  Florida Interactive Entertainment Academy (FIEA)

  Orlando, FL

  https://fiea.ucf.edu/

  Offers: Master's of Science in Interactive Entertainment

- **University of Utah**

  Entertainment Arts & Engineering

  Salt Lake City, Utah

  https://games.utah.edu/

  Offers: Bachelor of Science in Games; Bachelor of Science in Computer Science with an Entertainment Arts & Engineering Emphasis; Master of Entertainment Arts & Engineering; Dual Masters degrees in Entertainment Arts & Engineering (MEAE) and Business Administration (MBA)

- **University of Washington**

  Professional & Continuing Education

  Seattle, Washington

  https://www.pce.uw.edu/certificates/game-design

  Offers: Certificate in Game Design

For Profit, Private Colleges/Universities

- **DigiPen Institute of Technology**

  Redmond, WA; Singapore; Bizkaia, Spain

  https://www.digipen.edu/about

  Offers: Bachelor of Fine Arts in Game Design; Bachelor of Science in Computer Science and Game Design; Master of Fine Arts in Digital Arts

- **Full Sail University**

  Game School

  Orlando, FL

  https://www.fullsail.edu/area-of-study/games

  Offers: Bachelor of Science in Game Art; Bachelor of Science in Game Design; Bachelor of Science in Game Development; Bachelor of Science in Simulation & Visualization; Master of Science in Game Design; Master of Science in Mobile Gaming

References

"34th Annual Creative Arts & Entertainment Emmy Awards Presented at Star-Studded Hollywood Gala." (2007, June 14). Retrieved from emmyonline.com/day_34th_creaitve_winners

Aristotle. (1996). *Poetics*. London, UK: Penguin Books Ltd.

Ault, Susanne. (2014, August 5). *Variety.com* – "Survey: YouTube Stars More Popular Than Mainstream Celebs Among U.S. Teens." Retrieved from https://variety.com/2014/digital/news/survey-youtube-stars-more-popular-than-mainstream-celebs-among-u-s-teens-1201275245/

Berger, Ross. (2018, February 2). "Game Writer's Dilemma: Context vs. Story." *Encyclopedia of Computer Graphics and Games*. Retrieved from https://link.springer.com/referenceworkentry/10.1007/978-3-319-08234-9_129-1

Campbell, Joseph. (1991). *The Power of Myth*. New York: Anchor.

Cavalli, Earnest. (2007, November 20). "Halo Novel Becomes NYT Best Seller, Just Like My Novel Jurassic Park." Retrieved from https://www.destructoid.com/halo-novel-becomes-nyt-best-seller-just-like-my-novel-jurassic-park-55076.phtml

Chatfield, Tom. (2009, September 27). "Videogames Now Outperform Hollywood Movies." Retrieved from https://www.theguardian.com/technology/gamesblog/2009/sep/27/videogames-hollywood

Despain, Wendy. (2007, August 3). "Narrative Design for Company of Heroes: Stephen Dinehart on Writing for Games." Retrieved from http://www.gamasutra.com/view/feature/1530/narrative_design_for_company_of_.php

Egri, Lajos. (1942, 1946, 1960). *The Art of Dramatic Writing*. New York: Touchstone.

Elberse, Anita. (2013). *Blockbusters: Hit-making, Risk-taking, and the Big Business of Entertainment*. New York: Henry Holt and Co.

"God of War." (2018, April). Retrieved from https://www.playstation.com/en-us/games/god-of-war-ps4/

"Halo 3." (n.d.) Retrieved from http://www.vgchartz.com/game/6964/halo-3/?region=All

"Halo." (n.d.) Retrieved from https://vgsales.fandom.com/wiki/Halo

Jenkins, Henry. (2006). *Convergence Culture*. New York and London, UK: New York University Press.

"John Carter of Mars." (2012, June). Retrieved from https://www.the-numbers.com/movie/John-Carter-of-Mars#tab=video-sales

Jung, Carl. (1969). *The Archetypes and the Collective Unconscious* (Second edition). New York: Princeton University Press.

"The Last of Us." (2013, June 14). Retrieved from https://www.metacritic.com/game/playstation-3/the-last-of-us

"Motion Capture." (n.d.) Retrieved from https://en.wikipedia.org/wiki/Motion_capture

Sarkar, Samit. (2018, June 14). "The Last of Us Sales Tops 17 Million Copies Across PS3 and PS4." Retrieved from https://www.polygon.com/2018/6/14/17465488/the-last-of-us-sales-17-million-ps3-ps4

"Shadow of the Colossus." (2018, February 6). Retrieved from https://www.metacritic.com/game/playstation-4/shadow-of-the-colossus

Shanley, Patrick. (2019, January 16). "'Fortnite' Earned $2.4 Billion on 2018." Retrieved from https://www.hollywoodreporter.com/heat-vision/fortnite-earned-24-billion-2018-1176660

Shieber, Jonathan. (2019, January). "Video Game Revenue Tops $43 Billion in 2018, an 18% Jump from 2017." Retrieved from https://techcrunch.com/2019/01/22/video-game-revenue-tops-43-billion-in-2018-an-18-jump-from-2017/

Strowbridge, C.S. (2012, June 20). "Blu-ray Sales: John Carter Acts Up." Retrieved from https://www.the-numbers.com/news/128220830-Blu-ray-Sales-John-Carter-Acts-Up

"Video Game Console." (n.d.) Retrieved from https://en.wikipedia.org/wiki/Video_game_console

"The X-Files." (1998). Retrieved from https://www.boxofficemojo.com/movies/?id=x-filesfightthefuture.htm

About the Author

Ross Berger started his writing career as a playwright in New York, where he received the Cherry Lane Mentorship Fellowship, the Dramatists Guild Playwriting Fellowship, and the Ensemble Studio Theatre's Next-Step Fellowship. In 2004, he co-wrote the Emmy-submitted Sweeps Week episode "Gov Love" for NBC's *Law & Order*.

Since 2007, his career has been part Hollywood and part Silicon Valley. Ross bridges the gap between the two by designing, writing, and producing story experiences across traditional and new media platforms. Credits include the Webby Award-winning *lonelygirl15* (2007–2008), the *Obama Girl* franchise (2007–2008), and Go90's highest-rated show *The Runner* (2016). In the video game industry, Ross was the senior narrative designer for Microsoft Studios and Electronic Arts for such titles as *Quantum Break* (2016), *Sunset Overdrive* (2014), and the *NBA Live* franchise (2017–2018). Ross' first console title was *CSI: Deadly Intent* (2009), where he learned video game storytelling from the former masters of game narrative, Telltale Games. (Rest in peace.)

Ross has also worked extensively in Virtual Reality as a writer for the Oculus Rift launch title *Farlands* (2016) and for the award-winning *Eclipse: Edge of Light* (2017).

Ross is also a published author, a former animation writer, and a one-time scenario writer of a board game. A graduate of Brandeis (BA, Philosophy) and Columbia (MFA, Playwriting) universities, Ross is a member of the Writers Guild of America and the Television Academy.

Index

Printed in the United States
by Baker & Taylor Publisher Services